UNTER - UNDER

GROESSER~ BIG

ahs - on

Tsu - TO

FUN - FROM

A BROCN TSU DIR

MER

UN - AND

ZOG A POR VERTER*

ON - WITHOUT

*Say a few words! Curses, ribaldry and maxims are all included in this quick and easy phonetic guide to the world's most colorful language.

This is the first time that Yiddish has been presented in transliterated phonetic form, utilizing the Roman alphabet in place of Hebrew characters, so that every one can become a Yiddish *maven* instantly.

One word in Yiddish has so much more meaning than a dozen in any other language . . . so be a *mentsh* and *zog a por verter!*

NIT - NOTHING

TOG - DAY

SHAINEH- PRETTY

RAINEU - PURE

A Dictionary Of Yiddish Slang & Idioms

by Fred Kogos

PAPERBACK LIBRARY

New York

PAPERBACK LIBRARY EDITION
First Printing: February, 1969

This Paperback Library Edition is published
by arrangement with The Citadel Press.

*Paperback Library is a division of Coronet Communications,
Inc. Its trademark, consisting of the words "Paperback Library"
accompanied by an open book, is registered in the United States
Patent Office.* Coronet Communications, Inc., 315 Park Avenue
South, New York, N.Y. 10010.

INTRODUCTION:

WHY YIDDISH SLANG AND IDIOMS?

The success of our first effort to preserve Yiddish, called *Instant Yiddish,* was so great that it prompted the author to continue with his work. When Hitler killed 6,000,000 Yiddish-speaking Jews and when Israel proclaimed in 1948 that Hebrew was to be the official tongue of the nation, these actions spelled the death-knell of Yiddish. This was the pity of it all! And this the author did not want to see, for since its beginnings in the 11th century, Yiddish has been the mother tongue, the "mameh-loshen," of millions of Jews throughout Europe who eventually carried it throughout the world as they migrated to the United States, Canada, Latin America, Africa, Australia, and elsewhere. Yiddish, rather than Hebrew, was and is the language of communication among Jews —in common life, in stories, jokes, books, newspapers, the theatre and truly the Esperanto of the Western World. And—through its colorfulness, its target-accurate phrases, idioms and sayings—it exudes an aroma and a texture of refreshing magic and laughter as well as sober thought that has been handed down through the ages from generation to generation and country to country. The author is obsessed with the thought that with the loss of Yiddish, the Jews lose not merely a language, but the Jewish people! Hebrew is spoken only by about 2,000,000 people in Israel and a few abroad, while Yiddish is still spoken by, and known to, over 10,000,000 throughout the world! Yiddish is creeping into the English language more startlingly than is apparent, with even Webster's Third International Dictionary containing over 500 Yiddish (and some Hebrew) words.

Because of the author's determination to perpetuate this picturesque language, he has spent several years studying, talking, learning, gathering and codifying words, phrases, greetings, colloquialisms, idioms, proverbs, etc., wading through the many dialects—God bless them and our people!—to unify and simplify them. Thus, for the first time since Roman letters began to be used in the English language, a *Dictionary of Yiddish Slang and Idioms,* which utilizes Roman letters instead of Hebrew characters, is presented for those in the English-speaking world who desire to learn and enjoy some Yiddish without the necessity of learning the Hebrew characters used in Yiddish. Consequently, anyone who reads English will be able to read and learn Yiddish phonetically and to explore the vast riches of Yiddish idioms, sayings, and colloquialisms found in this collection.

The author is a world traveler, having visited 70 countries and spoken Yiddish in most of them. He is not a writer by profession; he started this *Dictionary of Yiddish Slang and Idioms* as a hobby and it turned into an obsession and love. He claims no lexicographic background nor scholarly pretensions. His great hope is that this work will be a monument to an idea and a spirit, and that this "storehouse" of Yiddish words and phrases may help to perpetuate Yiddish and the enjoyment of it in everyday life. With *Instant Yiddish,* the author's first work, *Yiddish Slang and Idioms* will make you quite popular in these days when it is considered quite "in" to be bilingual and speak Yiddish, or at least know some appropriate and timely Yiddishisms—words, phrases or expressions.

If you grew up in a Yiddish-speaking home, you learned some of the language. If you grew up on the Lower East Side of New York, or in any other Jewish quarter in the United States, then you were handed an opportunity on a silver platter and you learned your Yiddish accidentally. But if you didn't get the chance and now want it, and you cannot afford the time to go to school but still want to get on the Yiddish bandwagon—then *Yiddish Slang and Idioms* is for you!

This work was written primarily for those who are unfamiliar with Yiddish and for those who once knew Yiddish but have forgotten it.

In transliterating the Yiddish words into English letters, we have simply written the Yiddish words phonetically as if they were English. So it will be quite easy for you to speak Yiddish instantly and make friends or influence sales, or put some variety into your conversation. Moreover, since Yiddish is so universal a language, this work will enable you to make yourself understood—and get along—anywhere in the world where Yiddish is spoken. And that means practically everywhere. *Enjoy!*

FACTS ABOUT YIDDISH

Yiddish is spoken by about 10,000,000 people throughout the world. It is widely used in Russia, Poland, Rumania, France, England and other European countries. In the United States and Canada, in Israel, South Africa and other African countries, in Latin America, in New Zealand and Australia and wherever else Eastern European Jews emigrated to, Yiddish survives as a spoken language—in the home, on the streets, in the theatre, in literature, newspapers and the entertainment field. There is at this moment a strong revival of Yiddish throughout the United States.

Yiddish, whose principal parent is Middle High German, is also related directly to English as well as to the Hebrew, Russian, and Polish languages, and enjoys borrowings from other languages and countries along the routes Jews have painfully travelled since the 11th century, when Yiddish was born.

There are four principal accents in Yiddish: Lithuanian, Ukrainian (Galicia), Polish, and Western (German). That's where you get Litvaks, Galitsyaners and other territorial nicknames for Jews. The essential difference between them lies in the pronunciation—whether broad, long or short. We have the same differences in accents in the United States: Southern, New England, Midwestern, New Yorkese—but we all understand each other. In this work we use the standard form, based simply on the usage of the majority. You'll be understood in any Yiddish-speaking environment.

YOU ALREADY KNOW LOTS OF YIDDISH

Since Yiddish is descended from Middle High German, which is related to the Saxon part of Anglo-Saxon, many of the short and common English words are more or less analogous to their Yiddish counterparts. Also, we have many cognate words whose roots both in English and Yiddish are alike or similar. Only their pronunciations makes it difficult to recognize them. But their presence will be of great help to you when you speak Yiddish, and humorously enough, if you mispronounce such cognate words, as you would in broken English, they will usually come out as perfect Yiddish. Here are a few: *vinter* (winter), *zinger* (singer), *zumer* (summer), *hant* (hand), *gut* (good), *epel* (apple), *broyt* (bread), *orem* (arm), *bahkan* (bake), *bod* (bath), *bord* (beard), *beis* (bite), *bruder* (brother), *breng* (bring), *hoys* (house), *putter* (butter), *kalt* (cold), *kiel* (cool), *kozineh* (cousin), *tochter* (daughter), *zin* (son), *fahl* (fall) and very many others, including numbers.

In addition to the above words which closely resemble English, about 500 other Yiddish words have become part of our everyday language in their original form and are found in Webster's Third International Dictionary. Among them are: *gezuntheit* (good health; also, bless you!), *kindergarten* (kindergarten), *schlemiel* (clumsy dope), *shlimazel* (unlucky person), *mazel* (luck), *shmo* (patsy), *kibbitz* (to meddle), *shikker* (drunkard), *shalom* (peace and hello), *tzimmes* (fruit compote, also in slang, "big deal"), *Bar Mitzvah* (confirmation), *gefilteh fish* (stuffed fish), *halavah* (candy made of crushed sesame seeds and honey), *kosher* (proper Jewish food; also, OK!), *mitzvah* (commandment, good deed), *bris* (circumcision), *shabbes* (sabbath), *meshugeh* (crazy), *mishmash* (a mess, confusion), *schlumpf* (sucker, patsy), *shnook* (a dolt), and many others.

10

Vowels:	Diphthongs:	Consonants:
a as in *father*	ai as in *say* or *main*	dz as in soun*ds*
e as in *bed*	ei as in *by* or *height*	g as in go
i as in *lit* or *beer*	oi or oy as in *boy*	ch as in lo*ch* (Scottish)
o as in *hot*	or *voice*	or Ba*ch* (German)
u as in *put*	When 2 other vowels	r soft with no trill
	are together,	ts as in pa*ts*
	pronounce them	tsh as in *ch*urch
	separately.	zh as in sei*z*ure

Also, a number of letters and words of prefixes are used interchangeably—Ahf and Oyf, Nit and Nisht, Oi and Oy, Oo and U, S and Z and Tsu and Tzu.

IMPORTANT NOTES ON PRONUNCIATION

Ahf and Oyf: There are a number of words, diphthongs and phonemes whose spellings represent the pronunciations of their locale—Russia, Poland, Germany, etc., so that sometimes the same word has two phonetic appearances; for example, "ahf" and "oyf." As the author heard them or himself used them, so he recorded them here. Although every effort was made for consistency within this work, the author felt compelled to retain these pronunciations which sounded so natural to the ear. The attuned ear will appreciate this, although the educated eye would prefer "oyf" to "ahf."

"H" after the vowel: In many cases the letter "h" has been added to a word after the vowel, as in "ahf," "bohmer," and so on. The purpose of this is simply to warn you to broaden the vowel and to tell you that it is short and shouldn't be pronounced as in English. If you pronounce "ahf," as in the English, "after," you're wrong! "Ahf" must rhyme with the "a" in "harvest."

"H" at the end of the word: The letter "h" has been added to many words that end in vowels to make sure that you pronounce that vowel as a separate syllable.

11

ABOUT ACCENT

In words of two syllables, the accent falls mostly on the first syllable. In words of three syllables or more the accent falls mostly on the second syllable. Often a word is lengthened by prefixes or suffixes. In that case, the original accent is retained.

I hope this is not too *ongepatshket* (confusing) for you!

HOW TO USE THIS BOOK

This work is easy to use. It is divided into two parts: Yiddish-English and English-Yiddish, and includes popular and familiar (at least to knowledgeable Yiddish-speaking Jews) as well as odd and peppery words, sayings, phrases, proverbs, colloquialisms, maxims, curses, maledictions, taboos, vulgarisms and obscenities. All are accompanied by the most applicable definitions and literal meanings so that you may understand more clearly the figures of speech, particularly in the idioms, slang, curses, and proverbs. Each word is in *transliterated* Yiddish phonetically recorded into the Roman alphabet, and all you have to do is pronounce as written, keeping the pronunciation guide in mind.

The choices included are based on the author's personal life, research and extensive reading. But more important, this book represents the help and suggestions of hundreds of the author's friends throughout the world, to whom he is happily indebted and gratefully appreciative.

This book will prepare you for everyday life experiences by giving you Yiddish expressions that are constantly used in conversation so that you will be able to understand and be understood. And this holds true not only for the United States but abroad as well.

Yiddish is becoming so universal these days that knowing a little of it will facilitate daily contacts with Jews in your travels at home and abroad, help you in emergencies, make friends for you and give you altogether a pleasant feeling and a fascinating adventure. "For gezunterhait" (bon voyage) and "shalom alaichem" (peace be unto you)—and above all, "mazel tov" (good luck to you)!

YIDDISH-ENGLISH

A bisel A little

A biseleh A very little

A braireh hob ich? Do I have a choice?

A braiteh daieh hoben To do all the talking (Lit., To have the greatest say or authority)

A broch! Oh hell! Damn it! A curse!

A broch tsu dir! A curse on you!

A broch tsu mir! Woe is me! I have been cursed! (Lit., A curse to me!)

A brocheh A blessing

A choleryeh ahf dir! A plague on you!

A chazer bleibt a chazer! A pig remains a pig!

A chissoren, di kaleh iz tsu shain! Too bad that the bride is too pretty (Said of a novel or unjustified complaint)

A dank Thanks, thank you

A deigeh hob ich I don't give a hang. I don't care. I should worry.

A deigeh hob ich? Is it my worry?

A farshlepteh krenk A chronic ailment; particularly a lingering one

A feier zol im trefen He should burn up!

A gezunt ahf dein kop! Good health to you (Lit., Good health on your head)

A gezunt dir in pupik! Thanks for a small favor! (Lit., Good health to your belly button!)

A glick ahf dir! Good luck to you (Sometimes used sarcastically about minor good fortunes) Big thing!

A glick hot dir getrofen! Big deal! (Sarcastic; lit., A piece of luck happened to you!)

A klog iz mir! Woe is me!

A klog tzu meineh sonim! A curse on my enemies!

A lebedikeh velt Happy-go-lucky people (Lit., A lively world)

A leben ahf dir! You should live! (And be well—and have much more!)

A lek un a shmek A worker who does his job insufficiently gives this; you get this when a hostess serves peanut-size hors d'oeuvres—and too few of them; neither here nor there (Lit., A taste and a smell)

A lung un leber oyf der noz Stop talking yourself into illness! (Lit., Don't imagine a lung and a liver upon the nose)

A magaifeh zol dich trefen! A plague on you!

A makeh unter yenem's orem iz nit shver tzu trogen. Another man's disease is not hard to endure (Lit., A boil under another's arm is not hard to bear)

A mentsh on glik is a toyter mensh An unlucky person is a dead person (Lit., A man without luck is a dead man)

A metsieh fun a ganef It's a steal (Lit., A bargain from a thief)

A nar filt nit! A fool feels nothing!

A nar veist men nit kain halbeh arbet You don't show a fool something half-finished

A nechtiker tog! Finished! Gone! Fait accompli! Impossible! Nonsense (Lit., A yesterday's day)

A nishtikeit! A nobody!

A sach tsu reden, vainik tsu herren A lot to tell, little to hear

A shaineh, raineh, kaporeh Serves him (her) right! (Lit., A nice, pure sacrificial fowl)

A shainem dank dir in pupik! Thanks for nothing (Lit., Many thanks in your belly button)

14

A shandeh un a charpeh   A shame and a disgrace

A shtik naches   A great joy (Lit., A piece or slice of pleasure)

A sof! A sof!   Let's end it! End it!

A yor mit a mitvoch   It will take a long, long time (till Doomsday) (Lit., A year and a Wednesday)

Abi gezunt!   As long as you're healthy!

Abi tsu zein mit dir   As long as I can be with you

Achrahyes   Responsible

Aderabeh-ve'aderabeh   By all means

Ahf meineh sonim gezogt!   It should happen to my enemies!

Ahf mir gezogt!   I wish it could be said about me!

Ahf mir gezogt gevorn!   It should happen to me!

Ahf tsi 'lehaches; (ahf tsu loches)   In spite of everything you do, it still comes out wrong

Ahf tsores   In trouble

Ahfen goniff brent dos hittel   A guilty conscience; A guilty person is always sensitive (Lit., On the head of a thief, burns his hat)

Ahntoisht   Disappointed

Ahntoishung   Disappointment

Ahzes ponim   Impudent fellow

Aidel   Cultured

Aidel gepatshkit   Finicky, super-critical

Aidim   Son-in-law

Ain klainikeit   Big deal (Derisive; lit., A small matter, A mere bagatelle)

Aiver butel   Getting senile; absent-minded; mixed up

Alaichem sholom   To you be peace (The answer or response to the customary salutation, sholom alaichem, Peace be unto you)

Alef-bais   Alphabet; the first two letters of the Jewish alphabet; the beginning; common knowledge; ABC's

Aleh meiles hot zi!   She has all the virtues!

Aleh shusters gaien borves   All shoemakers go barefoot

Alevei!   It should happen to me (to you)! Would that it comes true!

Alteh moid   Spinster, old maid

Alter bocher   Bachelor

15

Alter Kucker (taboo) A lecherous old man; a played-out person, even if young; a person unwilling to participate (abbreviated to A.K.)

Altvarg Decrepit person or thing

Amho'orets Ignoramus, boor, peasant (also spelled "amorets")

An ain unaintsikeh A one and only, rarity

An alteh machashaifeh An old witch

An alter bakahnter An old acquaintance

An alter trombenick An old wreck, an old bum

Antshuldik mir Excuse me.

Arbeh kanfess Sleeveless religious undershirt

Arein In, into; Come in!

Aribergechapt di mohs! Overdressed woman

Aroysgevorfeneh gelt Money thrown out; money wasted

Arumgeflickt! Milked! Plucked!

Arumgevolgert Wandered around; loafed

Arumloifer Street urchin; person who runs around

Az a yor ahf mir. I should have such good luck. (Lit., Such a year to me)

Az drei zogen meshugeh, darf der ferter zogen "Bim bom." The majority rules. (Lit., If three people say or do something screwy, the fourth has to go along.)

Az es klingt, iz misstomeh chogeh. When people talk about something, it is probably true. (Lit., when bells ring, it is usually a holiday.)

Az och un vai! Tough luck! Too bad! Misfortune!

Azoy? Really?

Azoy gait es! That's how it goes! So it goes!

Azoy gich? So soon?

Azoy iz es! That's how it is!

Azoy ret men tsu a taten? Is that how you talk to a father?

Azoy vert dos kichel tzekrochen! That's how the cookie crumbles!

Azoy zogstu! That's what you (pl.) say!

B

Ba'al gaiveh Conceited

Baba stories, bubba meisses Grandmother tales, fairy tales, inventions (See also bobbeh meisseh)

Badchan Jester, merry maker or master of ceremonies at a wedding; at the end of the meal he announces the presents, lifting them up and praising the giver and the gift in a humorous manner

Bagel Hard circular roll with a hole in the center (like a doughnut) and a glazed surface

Bagroben To bury; buried

Baitsim (taboo) Testicles; eggs (The proper word for eggs is aier)

Baizeh chei-eh Vicious animal (usually refers to an inhumane person)

Balagoleh Teamster, waggoner, coachman, driver; vulgar man, one without manners

Balebatish Fine, responsible, honorable

Balebatisheh yiden Respectable Jews, men of substance and good standing in the community

Balebatishkeit Household, property, substance

Balebos Owner, the big boss; an orderly person, householder, head of family

Balebosteh Housewife, hostess, capable homemaker (complimentary)

17

Balmelocheh Artisan, skilled worker, mechanic

Balnes Miracle-worker

Bal shem Term applied to a faith-healer, magic-worker, miracle performer

Bal Simcheh One who celebrates a happy occasion

Bal Toyreh Learned man, scholar

Bal tsedokeh Benefactor, philanthropist

Barabantshik Drummer in a band

Bareden yenem To gossip

Baren (taboo) Fornicate; bother, annoy

Bareh mich nit Don't bother me. Don't screw me around!

Bareh nit (taboo) Don't fornicate around; don't fool around; don't annoy; don't bother (someone)

Barimer Braggart, show-off

Bar-mitzvah Boy who, upon the completion of his thirteenth year, accepts the responsibility of fulfilling the religious law; also the celebration of this event, of becoming a man (Lit., Son of commandment)

Baroygis Angry, petulant

Bas Daughter (Hebrew)

Bas-mitzvah Girl who has reached the age when she is required to fulfill certain mitzvos (commands, obligations); the coming of age; a woman

Bashert Fated

Bashert zein To be destined

Basherter Beloved; the fated one, the destined one

Bas-malkeh Princess (Lit., Daughter of a queen)

Batlen Egghead (Talmudic)

Baveibter Married man (veib means wife)

Beblech Beans

Behaimeh Animal, cow (when referring to human being, means dull-witted or a fool)

Bei mir poilst du It's O.K. with me

Ben Son (Hebrew); zun, Yiddish

Ben toyreh Learned man, scholar (Lit., Son of the Torah)

Bentshen lecht Recite benedictions over lit candles on Sabbath eve and holidays

Bentshing Anglicization of Yiddish word bentshen, to say grace

18

Beryeh   Efficient, competent housewife

Bes medresh   Synagogue

Billik   Cheap, inexpensive

Billik vi borsht!   Cheap as beet soup! A real bargain! A real buy!

Bist ahf ain fus?   Are you in a hurry? (Lit., Are you standing on one leg?)

Bist meshugeh?   Are you carzy?

Biteh   Please

Blaich vi di vant   Pale as a sheet (wall)

Blintses   Cheese or jellied pancakes rolled in dough and fried in fat (The French call it crêpe suzette)

Blondjen   To wander; be lost, as in the woods or on strange roads

Blozen fun zich   Puffed with haughty pride; shows off

Bobbeh meisseh   Grandmother story (Figuratively, a fairy tale, an unbelievable story, a tall story)

Bobkes   Small things, triflings, peanuts, nothing, worthless (Lit., Excreta of sheep, goats)

Bocher   Bachelor, unmarried man, young man

Bohmer   Bum (masc., Americanism)

Bohmerkeh   Bum (fem., Americanism)

Boitshick   Little boy; affectionate term for boy or man (Americanism)

Bordel   Brothel, whorehouse

Borsht   Beet or cabbage soup

Borsht circuit   Hotels in the Catskill Mountains, New York, with an almost entirely Jewish clientele, who are fond of borsht (beet and potato soup); term is used by entertainers

Boruchu (Hebrew)   Bless ye

Boruch hashem (Hebrew)   Bless God!

Borves   Barefoot

Botshvineh   Spinach soup

Boych vaitik   Stomach ache

Brahv   Brave

Braiter vi lainger   He's so happy! (Lit., Wider than longer, as with a big wide smile)

Brech a fus!   Break a leg!

Bris   Circumcision; the ceremony of circumcision

Bris Mieleh   Circumcision

19

Bristen   Breasts, teats

Broch   Fracture, break (Figuratively, a curse)

Broitgeber   Head of family

Bronfen   Whiskey

Brust   Breast

B'suleh   Virgin

B'suleh-shaft   Virginity

B'sulim   Hymen

Bubbee (booh-bee)   Friendly term for anybody you like

Bubeleh   Endearing term for anybody you like, young or old

Bubkes   Beans; a mere bagatelle; (Slang, see Bobkes)

Buba   Insignificant mistake

Bulvan   Man built like an ox; boorish, coarse, rude person

Burtchet   Growled

Cancer-shmancer, abi gezunt Cancer-shmancer, as long as you're healthy!

Chaleshen To faint

Challah Sabbath twists of white bread (Made in a variety of forms for the various holidays of the year)

Chaloshes Weakness, nausea, faintness, unconsciousness

Chamoyer du ainer! You blockhead! You dope! You donkey! You ass!

Chanifeh Over-praise

Chap a gang! Beat it! (Lit., Catch a way, catch a road)

Chap nit! Take it easy! Not so fast! (Lit., Don't grab)

Chas v'cholileh! God forbid! Not really at all!

Chaver (pl., Chavairim) Friend, Mr., comrade, colleague

Chaverteh Friend (fem.), Mrs., Miss, Companion

Chazen Cantor

Chazenteh Wife of chazen

Chazzer Pig, a piggish person

Chazzerei Swill; pig's feed; anything bad, unpalatable, rotten

Chei Eighteen; life; word formed by the combination of Hebrew letters meaning eighteen and life

Chei(im) Life; (Le'cheiim (to life) is used as a toast equal to Here's to you, Skol, Down the hatch, etc. Cheiim is also a favorite name among Jews, becoming

21

Hyman, later Henry, Herbert and other variations)

Chei kuck (Taboo) Nothing, infiintesimal, worthless, unimportant (Lit., human dung)

Chevreh Company, society, associates

Chmalyeh! Bang, punch; Slam! Wallop!

Chochem Wise man; (slang) a wise guy

Chochem attick A wise guy

Chochmeh Wisdom, bright saying, witticism (often sarcastically)

Cholileh! God forbid! Perish the thought!

Choleryeh Cholera; a curse, plague

Choshever mentsh Man of worth and dignity; elite person; respected person

Chosid Rabid fan

Chossen Bridegroom

Chossen-kalleh Bride and groom; engaged couple

Chosser daieh Feeble-minded

Choyzik machen Make fun of, ridicule

Chropen Snore

Chupeh Bridal canopy (Its four poles signify the four corners of the world, and support a blue cloth, symbolic of the heavens); the marriage ceremony itself

Chutzpeh Brazenness, gall, cheek

Chutzpenik Impudent fellow

Christiyah Enema

Cristiyer Enema

Danken Got! Thank God!

Davenen Pray

Davening mincheh Recite the afternoon or mincheh prayers, which consist of selections from psalms plus the Sh'moneh Esrei (Eighteen Benedictions) (Note English suffix "ing." The verb is davenen.)

Deigeh nisht! Don't worry!

Den Adverb used with questions to connote about (for example: "vo den?" for what else? "vi den" for how else?); then

Der oybershter in himmel God (Lit., The One above in heaven)

Derech erets Respect

Derniderriken Berate, to humble somebody

Dershtikt zolstu veren! You should choke on it!

Di emmeseh schoireh! The real article!

Dingen Bargain, hire, engage, lease, rent

Dos gefelt mir This pleases me

Dos gelt iz tserunen gevoren! My money went down the drain!

Dos hartz hot mir gezogt My heart told me. I predicted it.

Dos iz alts That's all

Dos iz geven a mechei-eh This was a pleasure!

Dos zelbeh Likewise.

23

Drai mir nit kain kop! Don't bother me! (Lit., Don't twist my head)

Drai zich! Keep moving!

Draikop Scatterbrain; one who tends to confuse you; one who connives and twists the facts to serve his own purpose (Lit., turn-head)

Drek (taboo) Human dung, feces, manure or excrement; inferior merchandise or work; insincere talk or excessive flattery

Drek ahf a shpendel (taboo) As unimportant as dung on a piece of wood

Du fangst shoyn on? Are you starting up again?

Dumkop Dumbbell, dunce (Lit., Dumb head)

Dybbuk Soul condemned to wander for a time in this world because of its sins. (To escape the perpetual torments inflicted upon it by evil spirits, the dybbuk seeks refuge in the body of some pious man or woman over whom the demons have no power. The dybbuk is a Cabalistic conception)

Ech   A groan, a disparaging exclamation

Efsher   Maybe, could be

Ehe!   Nothing of importance (exclamation)

Ei! Ei!   Yiddish exclamation equivalent to the English "Oh!"

Ei, gut!   Great! Just great!

Eilt zich!   Get a move on! Hurry up! Rush!

Eingeshpahrt   Stubborn

Eingetunken   Dipped, dunked

Einhoreh   Evil eye

Eizel   Fool, dope

Ek velt   End of the world

Ekeldiker parshoya   Disgusting fellow

El, eleh   Suffixes denoting diminutive or affection

Emes   Truth; on the level, on the square

Er bolbet narishkeiten.   He talks nonsense

Er drait zich vi a fortz in rossel! (taboo)   Is he bewildered! Is he in a fog! (Lit., he squirms like a fart in a foggy soup)

Er est vi noch a krenk.   He eats as if he just recovered from a sickness

Er farkocht a kasheh.   He makes a mess.

Er frest vi a ferd.   He eats like a horse.

Er hot a farshtopten kop.   He's thick headed.

Er hot a farshtopteh nonyeh. He has a cold. He has a stuffed nose.

Er hot a makeh. He has nothing at all (Lit., He has a boil or a minor hurt.)

Er hot kadoches. He has nothing. (Lit., Malaria fever (ague) is all that he gets!)

Er hot modneh drochim. He has odd ways.

Er hot nit kain daieh. He has no say (authority).

Er hot nit kain zorg. He hasn't got a worry.

Er iz a niderrechtiker kerl! He's a low down good-for-nothing.

Er iz shoyn du, der nudnik! The nuisance is here already!

Er kert iber di velt! He turns the world upside down!

Er kricht in di hoyecheh fenster. He aspires to high places (beyond his reach); a social climber (Lit., He creeps on high windows.)

Er kricht oyf di gleicheh vent. Trouble-maker; a man who criticizes things that don't exist or that are uncriticizable (Lit., He climbs up straight walls.)

Er kricht vi a vantz. He's slow as molasses. (Lit., He creeps like a bedbug.)

Er kukt vi a hun in a B'nai Odom. He doesn't know what he's looking at.

Er macht a tel fun dem. He ruins it.

Er macht mir a shvartzeh chasseneh! He makes a lot of trouble for me! (Lit., He makes my wedding black.)

Er molt gemolen mel. He repeats himself. He re-hashes things over and over again. (Lit., He grinds ground flour.)

Er redt in der velt arein! He talks nonsense! (Lit., He talks into the world.)

Er redt zich ein a krenk! He talks himself into a sickness!

Er zitst oyf shpilkes. He's restless. (Lit., He sits on pins and needles.)

Er toyg ahf kapores. He's worthless. (Lit., He's good only for a fowl sacrifice.)

Er zol einemen a mieseh meshuneh! He should go to hell! (Lit., He should meet with a strange death.)

Er zol vaksen vi a tsibeleh, mit dem kop in drerd! He

26

should grow like an onion, with his head in the ground!

Eretz Yisroel. Land of Israel.

Es brent mir ahfen hartz. I have a heartburn.

Es cholemt zich mir . . . I am dreaming that . . .

Es gait nit! It doesn't work! It isn't running smoothly!

Es gefelt mir. I like it. (Lit., It pleases me.)

Es hot zich oysgelohzen a boydem! Nothing came of it! (Lit., There's nothing up there but a small attic.)

Es iz a shandeh far di kinder! It's a shame for the children!

Es iz bloteh. There's nothing. That's worthless. It's nothing. (Lit., It is mud).

Es iz mir eingefalen a plan. A plan occurred to me.

Es iz nit geshtoigen un nit gefloigen! It never happened! It doesn't make sense! (Lit., It was never standing and never flying.)

Es iz noch do There still is

Es iz (tsu) shpet. It is (too) late.

Es iz vert a zets in drerd! It is as futile as stomping on the earth! (Lit., It's [not even] worth a knock on the earth.)

Es iz zaier teier (billik). It is very expensive (cheap).

Es ken gemolt zein. It is conceivable. It is imaginable.

Es kein zein. It could be.

Es ligt im (ir) in zinnen. It's on his (her) mind.

Es ligt im nit in zinnen. He doesn't give a damn. (Lit., It's not on his mind.)

Es macht mir nit oys. It doesn't matter to me.

Es macht nit oys. It makes no difference. It doesn't matter. It isn't important.

Es past nit. It is not becoming. It is not fitting.

Es past zich vi a patsh tsu gut shabbes! It's bad manners. It's not to the point. (Lit., It fits like a slap in the face in response to the greeting: Good Sabbath.)

Es tut mir a groisseh hanoeh! It gives me great pleasure! (often said sarcastically)

Es tut mir bahng. I'm sorry. (Lit., It sorrows me)

Es tut mir laid. I'm sorry.

Es tut mir vai. It hurts me.

Es veist zich mir oys It appears to me

27

Es vert mir finster in di oygen. I am fainting! (Lit., It's getting dark in my eyes.)

Es vet gornit helfen! Nothing will help!

'Es vet helfen vi a toiten bahnkes! It won't help (any)! (Lit., It will help like blood-cupping on a dead body.)

Es vet kleken. This will do. It will suffice.

Es vet zich alles oyspressen. It will all work out.

Es vet zich oys-hailen far der chasseneh. It will heal in time for the wedding. (Told even to a child when it gets hurt. The implication is that marriage is a cure-all.)

Es zhumit mir in kop. There's a buzzing in my head.

Ess gezunterhait! Eat in good health!

Essen mitik Dine

Essen teg Yeshiva students would arrange to be fed by various householders on a daily basis in different houses. (Lit., Eat days)

Faigeleh Little bird. Also, a pervert, fairy, homosexual, fag

Fang shoyn on! You may start now! Come on, get going!

Fangst shoyn on? Are you beginning again? Are you starting something?

Farantvortlech Responsible

Fantazyor Man who builds castles in the air

Farbissener Embittered; bitter person

Farblondzhet Lost, bewildered, confused

Farblujet Bending your ear

Farbrenter Rabid fan, ardent participant

Fardart Dried

Fardeiget Distressed, worried, full of care, anxiety

Fardinen a mitzveh Earn a blessing or a merit (by doing a good deed)

Fardrai zich dem kop! Go drive yourself crazy!

Fardrai zich dein eigenem kop vestu mainen s'iz meiner! Go drive yourself crazy, then you'll know how I feel! (Lit., Turn your own head around, and you'll think it's mine)

Fardross Disappointment, sorrow

Farein Society

Farfel Noodle dough, grated or chopped into barley-sized grains

29

Farfolen Lost

Farfoylt Mildewed, rotten, decayed

Farfroyren Frozen

Fargenigen Pleasure

Farglust Have a yen for

Farkuckt (taboo) Dungy, shitty

Farmach dos moyl! Shut up! Quiet. (Lit., Shut your mouth.)

Farmatert Tired

Farmish nit di yoytzres! Don't mix things up! (Lit., don't mix up the holiday prayers.)

Farmisht Mixed up emotionally; befuddled

Farmutshet Worn out, fatigued, exhausted

Farnem zich fun danen! Beat it!

Farshlepteh krenk Fruitless, endless matter (Lit., A sickness that hangs on)

Farshmeieter Highly excitable person; always on the go

Farshnoshket Loaded, drunk

Farshtaist? You understand?

Farshtopt Stuffed up, cluttered

Farshtunken Smells bad, stinky

Farshvitst Sweaty

Fartrasket Decorated (beautified)

Far-tshadikt Confused, bewildered, befuddled, as if by fumes, gas

Farzorger Head of family

Feckuckteh (taboo) Dungy, shitty

Feh! Fooey!

Feinkochen Omelet, scrambled eggs

Feinshmeker Person with fine taste; elite, hi-falutin'

Ferd Horse, (slang) a fool

Fet Fat, obese

Filantrop Philanthropist

Filen zich opgenart Disappointed

Finf A $5 bill; five; fiver

Finferel $5 bill

Finster un glitshik Miserable (Lit., Dark and slippery)

(A) Finsteren sof Horrible ending (Lit., A dark ending)

(A) Finster yor! A curse! (Lit., A dark year)

(A) Finsternish Plague; a curse (Lit., Darkness, gloom)

Fisfinger Toes

Flaishik, (Flaishidik) Meat or meat ingredients (must not be eaten at the same meal with dairy, milechik, foods)

Focha Fan

Foigel Smart guy

Foiler Lazy man

Folg mich! Obey me!

Folg mich a gang! Quite a distance! Quite a job! Why should I do it? It's hardly worth the trouble! (Lit., Follow me on an errand.)

Folg mich a gang un gai in drerd! Do me a favor and drop dead!

Fonfen Speak through the nose. Unclear. To double talk.

(Er) fonfet unter He bluffs his way out

Fonfevateh Talking through the nose

For gezunterhait! Bon voyage! Travel in good health!

Forshpeiz Appetizer

Fortz (taboo) Fart, wind-passing, flatulence, eructation

Fortzen (taboo) Pass or break wind, flatulate, eructate

Frageh Question

Frailech Happy

Frassk Slap in the face

Freg mich becherim! Ask me another! How should I know? Who knows? (Lit., even if you excommunicate me, I cannot give you the answer.)

Freilein Miss, young lady

Freint Friend, Mr.

Fremder Stranger

Fressen Eat like a pig, devour

Fresser Big eater, gourmand

Fressing Gourmandizing (By adding the English suffix "ing" to the Yiddish word "fress," a new English word in the vocabulary of American Jews has been created.)

Froy Woman, Mrs.

Frum, (frimer) Pious, religious, devout

Fun eier moyl in Got's oyeren! God should hear you and do as you say! (Lit., from your mouth to God's ears)

Funfeh Speaker's fluff, error

Funfen Speak through the nose; unclear; to double-talk

G

Gai avek!   Go away!

Gai bareh di vantsen!   Go bother the bedbugs!

Gai fardrai zich dein aigenem kop!   Go drive yourself crazy! Go mix yourself up, not me! (Lit., Go twist your own head.)

Gai feifen ahfen yam!   Go peddle your fish elsewhere! (Lit., Go whistle on the ocean)

Gai gezunterhait!   Bon voyage! Good-bye. (Lit., go in good health.)

Gai in drerd arein!   Go to hell! (Lit., Go down into the earthly grave.)

Gai kabenyeh mattereh!   Go to hell (Slavism)

Gai klap zich kop in vant!   It's useless (Lit., Go bang your head against the wall.)

Gai kucken ahfen yam! (taboo)   Don't bother me! Get lost! (Lit., Go defecate on the ocean.)

Gai plats!   Go split your guts!

Gai shlog zich mit Got arum!   Go fight City Hall! (Lit., Go fight with God.)

Gai shoyn, gai.   Scram! also, Don't be silly!

Gai strasheh di gens!   You don't frighten me! (Lit., Go threaten the geese)

Gai tren zich. (taboo)   Go frig yourself!

Gaien tsu kind Going into labor to give birth.

Gait, gait! Come now!

Gait es nit! It doesn't work!

Galitsianer Jewish native of Galicia

Gam atem The same to you. (Hebrew)

Ganaiden Garden of Eden; Paradise

Ganef Crook, thief, burglar, swindler, racketeer

Grants gut Quite well

Gantseh megilleh Big deal! (derisive)

Gantser k'nacker! Big shot!

Gantser mentsh Manly, a whole man, a complete man; an adult; a fellow who assumes airs

Gatkes Long winter underwear

Gazlen Robber; criminal, racketeer, murderer

Geben shoychad To bribe

Gebentsht mit kinder Blessed with children

Gebrenteh tsores Utter misery

Gebrochener english Fractured English

Gechropet Snored

Gedainkst? Remember?

Gedarteh Dried

(Es) Gefelt mir I like it. It pleases me.

Geferlech Dangerous

Gefilteh fish Stuffed fish (Usually made of chopped fish, onions and seasoning, and cooked in salt water)

Gefilteh helsel Stuffed chicken-neck skin

Gefilteh kishkeh Stuffed derma (intestines)

Gehakteh english Fractured English

Gehakter hering Chopped herring

Gehakteh leber Chopped liver

Gehakteh tsores Utter misery (Lit., Chopped-up troubles.)

Geharget zolstu veren! Drop dead! (Lit., You should get killed.)

Gelaimter Person who drops whatever he touches

Gelibteh Beloved

Gelt Money

Gelt gait tzu gelt. Money goes to money.

Gembeh! Big mouth!

Gemitlich Slowly, unhurried, gently

33

Genaivisheh shtiklech Tricky, sharp, crooked actions or doings

Genug iz genug. Enough is enough!

Gesheft Business

Geshmak Tasty, delicious

Geshtank A stink, foul odor

Geshtroft Cursed, accursed; punished

Geshvollen Swollen, puffed up (Also applied to person with haughty pride)

Get Divorce

Gevaldikeh zach! A terrible thing! (often ironically)

Gevalt! See G'vald

(A) Gezunteh moid! Brunhilde, a big healthy dame

Gezunt vi a ferd Strong as a horse

Gezunterhait In good health

Gezunt-heit! Good health! (Use when someone sneezes or as a toast!)

Gib mir nit kain einoreh! Don't give me a canary! (Americanism, Lit., Don't give me an evil eye)

Gib zich a shockel. Get a move on.

Gib zich a traisel Get a move on

Gleichtseitik Likewise, simultaneously

Gleichvertel Wisecrack, pun, saying, proverb, bon mot, witticism

Gleichvort Proverb

Glezel tai Glass of tea

Glezeleh varems Tea (Lit., A glass of warmth)

Glick Luck, piece of luck

Gloib mir! Believe me!

Glusten tsu To have a yen for

G'nossen tsum emess! The sneeze confirmed the truth!

Goilem Dull person; clumsy and sluggish; mechanical man, robot

Goldeneh chasseneh Fiftieth wedding anniversary

Goldeneh medineh Golden country (meaning the United States)

Goniff Thief, same as ganef

Gornisht Nothing

Gornit Nothing

Got di neshomeh shuldik Innocent (Lit., All he owes is his soul to God)

34

Got hit op di naronim God watches out for or protects the fools

Got in himmel! God in heaven! (said in anguish, despair, fear or frustration)

Got tsu danken Thank God

Got vaist God knows

Got vet shtrofen God will punish

Got zol ophiten! God forbid!

Gotteniu! Oh God! (anguished cry)

Goy Gentile; non-observant Jew; a Jew unfamiliar with Judaism

Goyeh Gentile woman

Goyisher kop Used in Eastern Europe to imply slow-wittedness

Greps Belch; a burp if it's a mild one

Gribbenes (grivvenes, greeven) Small crisp pieces left from rendered poultry fat or skin, fried and eaten as a delicacy or combined with kasha groats or rice; cracklings

Grizhen mit di tsain To grind one's teeth

Grizhidiker Gnawing, grinding person

Grob Coarse, crude, gross, profane, rough, rude

Grober Coarse, uncouth, crude; blasphemous person

Grober finger Thumb

(A) Grober yung (See Gruber yung)

Grobyungish Vulgar

Grois-halter Show-off, conceited person

Grois vi a barg As large as a mountain

Groisseh gedilleh! Big deal! (said sarcastically)

Groisseh metsieh Big bargain

Groisser fardiner! Big breadwinner! (sarcastically said of person who isn't) (Lit., big earner)

Groisser gornisht Big good-for-nothing

Groisser k'nacker! Big shot! Big wheel!

Groisser potz! (taboo) Big penis! Big prick! Big fool! Big shot! (Deragatory or sarcastic)

Groisser shisser Big shot, big wheel

Gruber yung Uncouth, rude, boorish young man

Gut far him! Serves him right!

Gut Shabbes Good Sabbath

Gut Yontev Good Holiday

35

Guten tog Good day; good-bye
Guts, (gits) Good things—food, dollars, news, etc.
G'vald! Cry of distress for help; wail of sorrow (Lit., Force, violence)
G'vir Rich man

Hadassah Jewish women's organization which devotes itself to the maintenance of medical services in Israel (Hadassah means myrtle, a tree highly regarded by Israel of old; Hadassah became a favorite name for girls. Esther's name, as told in the Bible, was originally Hadassah. The women's organization bearing her name was founded on the Purim holiday of 1912)

Hagadah Book of services for the first two nights of Passover

Haimish ponem Friendly face, familiar face (from home)

Haiseh venneh Hot bath

Haken a tsheinik Boring, long-winded and annoying conversation; talking for the sake of talking (Lit., To bang on the tea-kettle)

Hak flaish Chopped meat

Hak mir nit in kop! Stop bending my ear (Lit., Stop banging on my head)

Hak mir nit kain tsheinik Don't bother me (Lit., Don't bang on the tea-kettle)

Haldz-shvenkechts Gargle solution

Halevei! Would that it came true!

Hamotzi lechem min ho'orets Blessing over bread (Hebrew) (Lit., Who bringeth forth bread from the earth)

Hamoyn   Common people

Handlen   To bargain; to do business

Hartsvaitik   Heart ache

Hartseniu!   Sweetheart, my heart's love

Heizel   Brothel

Hekdish   Decrepit place, a slumhouse, poorhouse; a mess

Heldish   Brave

Hert zich ein!   Listen here!

Hetsken zich   Shake and dance with joy

Hikevater   Stammerer

Hinten   Rear, rear parts, backside, buttocks; in the rear

Hit zich!   Look out!

Hit zich vi fun a feier!   Watch yourself as if a fire threatened!

Hitsik   Hothead

Hitskop   Excitable person

Hob derech erets   Have respect

Hob nit kain deiges   Don't worry

Hoben chaishek tsu   To have a yen for

Hoben tsu zingen un tsu zogen   Have no end of trouble (Lit., To have to sing and to talk)

Hoizer gaier   Beggar

Hoi-echer drong   Long lean person

Hoizirer   Peddler (from house to house)

Holebshess   Stuffed cabbage

Holishkes   Stuffed cabbage

Holubtshes   Stuffed cabbage

Host du bei mir an aveleh!   So I made a mistake. So what!

Hultei   Debauchee, person of loose morals

Hulyen   Raise Cain, to carouse

I HAVE YOU....
ICH HOB DICH
I HAVE HIM..
ICH HOB IM

Ich bin ahntoisht   I am disappointed
Ich bin dich nit mekaneh   I don't envy you
Ich darf es ahf kapores   It's good for nothing! I have no
   use for it. (Lit., I need it for a [useless] fowl sacrifice)
Ich darf es vi a lung un leber ahfen noz   I need it like a
   wart on my nose (Lit., . . . like a lung and liver on my
   nose)
Ich darf es vi a loch in kop!   I need it like a hole in the
   head!
Ich eil zich (nit)   I am (not) in a hurry
Ich feif oif dir!   I despise you! Go to the devil! (Lit., I
   whistle on you!)
Ich fil zich opgenart   I am disappointed. (Lit., I feel
   cheated.)
Ich hob dir!   Go flap your ears! Drop dead! Scram! (Lit.,
   I have you . . . !) (Americanism!)
Ich hob dich in bod!   I despise you! (Lit., I have you in
   the bath house!)
Ich hob dich in drerd!   I have you in hell! Go to hell!
   (Lit., I have you in the earth)
Ich hob es in drerd!   To hell with it!
Ich hob im feint   I hate him
Ich hob im in bod!   Forget him! The hell with him! (Lit.,
   I have him in the bath house)

39

Ich hob im in toches (taboo) "I have him in my buttocks." Usually said about someone you don't care for,
or are angry with.

Ich vais. I know.

Ich vais nit. I don't know.

Ich vel dir geben kadoches! I'll give you nothing! (Lit.,
I'll give you malaria or a fever.)

Ich yog zich nit. I'm not in a hurry.

Ich zol azoy vissen fun tsores. I should know as little
about trouble (as I know about what you are asking
me).

Iker Substance; people of substance

Ikevater Stammerer

In a noveneh For a change; once in a blue moon

In di alteh guteh tseiten! In the good old days!

In drerd mein gelt! My money went down the drain!
(Lit., My money went to burial in the earth, to hell.)

In miten drinen In the middle of; suddenly

Inten (hinten) Behind, fanny, buttocks (slang)

Ipish Bad odor, stink

Ir gefelt mir zaier. You please me a great deal.

Iz brent mir ahfen hartz. I have a heartburn.

Kaas (in kaas oyf)   Angry (with)

Kabaret forshtelung   Floorshow

Kabtzen, kaptsen   Pauper

Kabtzen in ziben poless   A very poor man (Lit., a pauper in seven edges)

Kaddish   Mourner's prayer, in praise of and submission to the will of God

Kaddishel   Baby son; endearing term for a boy or man (Derived from word "kaddish," which is a prayer for the dead that only males may recite)

Kadoches   Fever, malaria (Also means, ironically, less than nothing)

Kadoches mit koshereh fodem!   Absolutely nothing! (Lit., fever with kosher thread.)

Kaftan   Long coat worn by religious Jews

Kain ein horeh.   No evil eye! (Some say "don't give me a canary"; Lit., May no evil befall.)

Kakapitshi   Conglomeration

Kalamutneh   Dreary, gloomy, troubled

Kalleh moid   Girl of marriageable age

Kallehniu   Little bride

Kalyekeh   Cripple; misfit; also, anybody not good at their craft or sport

41

Kalyeh Bad, wrong, spoiled

Kam derlebt Narrowly achieved (Lit., hardly lived to see)

Kam* mit tsores! Barely made it! (Lit., with some troubles)

*The word "Kam," also is pronounced "Kom" or "Koim" depending on the region people come from.

Kam vos er kricht Barely able to creep; Mr. Slowpoke

Kam vos er lebt He's hardly (barely) alive.

Kamtsoness To be miserly

Kaneh Enema

Kaporeh, (kapores) Atonement sacrifice; forgiveness; (slang) good for nothing

Karabelnick Country peddler

Karger Miser, tightwad

Kasheh Groats, mush cereal, buckwheat, porridge; a mess, mix-up, confusion

Kasheh varnishkes Cooked groats and broad noodles

Kashress Kosher condition; Jewish religious dietary law

Kasnik, (keisenik) Angry person; excitable person, hot head

Kasokeh Cross-eyed

Katshkehdik (Americanism) Ducky, swell, pleasant

Katzisher kop Forgetful (Lit., Cat head)

Kazatskeh Lively Russian dance

Kemfer Fighter (usually for a cause)

Ken zein Maybe, could be

(To) Kibbitz To offer unsolicited advice as a spectator

Kibbitzer Meddlesome spectator

Kiddish (Borai pri hagofen) Blessing over wine or bread on the eve of the Sabbath or Festivals

Kimpet-tzettel Childbirth amulet or charm (from the German "kind-bet-tzettel" meaning childbirth label containing Psalm 121, names of angels, patriarchs

Kimpetoren Woman in labor or immediately after the delivery

Kinderlech Diminutive, affectionate term for children

Kind un kait Young and old

Kishef macher Magic-worker

Kishkeh Stuffed derma (Sausage shaped, stuffed with a mixture of flour, onions, salt, pepper and fat to keep it together, it is boiled, roasted and sliced)

(A) Kitsel Tickle

Klainer gornisht Little prig (Lit., A little nothing)

Klemt beim hartz Clutches at my heartstrings

Klaperkeh Talkative woman

Klipeh Gabby woman, shrew, a female demon

Klogmuter Complainer, chronic complainer

(A) Klog iz mir! Woe is me!

Klop Bang, a real hard punch or wallop

Klotz Ungraceful, awkward, clumsy person; bungler

Klotz kasheh Foolish question; fruitless question

Kloymersht Not in reality, pretended (Lit., as if it were)

K'nacker Big shot; show-off; wise guy (Be sure to pronounce the first k)

K'naidel (pl., k'naidlech) Round dumplings usually made of matzoh meal and cooked in soup

K'nippel Button, knot; hymen, virginity; money tied in a knot in the corner of handkerchief

K'nish (taboo) Vagina

K'nishes Baker dumplings filled with potato, meat, liver or barley

Kochalain Summer boarding house with cooking privileges (Lit., cook by yourself)

Kochedik Petulant, excitable

Kochleffel One who stirs up trouble; gadabout, busybody (Lit., a cooking ladle)

Kolboynik Rascally know-it-all

(A) Kop oif di plaitses! Good, common sense! (Lit., A head on the shoulders!)

Kopvaitik Headache

Kosher Food that meets rules of Jewish dietary laws; (slang) right, perfect, clean, proper

Kosher v'yosher! It's perfect! (Lit., It's legitimate.)

Kosokeh Cross-eyed

Koved Respect, honor, reverence, esteem

Krank Sick

Krank-heit Sickness

Krassavitseh · Beauty, a doll, beautiful woman

Krechts Groan, moan

Krechtser Blues singer, a moaner

Krenk Sickness, disease

Kreplach Small pockets of dough filled with chopped meat or cheese which look like ravioli, or won ton soup, and are eaten in soup; (slang) nothing, valueless

Kroivim Relatives

Kuck im on (taboo) Defecate on him! The hell with him!

Kuck zich oys! (taboo) Go take a shit for yourself!

Kucken (taboo) To defecate

Kucker (taboo) Defecator, shit-head

Kuckteppel (taboo) Pot to defecate in

Kugel Noodle or bread suet pudding, frequently cooked with raisins

Kuck im on! Look at him!

Kum ich nit heint, kum ich morgen. Mañana! Procrastinating (Lit., If I don't come today, I'll come tomorrow.)

Kumen tsu gast To visit

Kuntzen Tricks

Kuntzen macher Magic worker, trickster

Kunyehlemel Naive, clumsy, awkward person; nincompoop; Casper Milquetoast

Kurveh Whore, prostitute

Kush in toches arein! (taboo) Kiss my behind! (said to somebody who is annoying you)

Kush mich in toches! (taboo) Kiss my behind! Stop annoying me.

Kushinyerkeh Cheapskate; woman who comes to a store and asks for five cents' worth of vinegar in her own bottle

K'vatsh Boneless person, one lacking character; a whiner, weakling

K'velen Glow with pride and happiness, beam; be delighted

K'vetsh Whine, complain; whiner, a complainer

K'vitsh Shriek, scream, screech

ㄥ

Lachen mit yash-tsherkes Forced or false laugh; laugh
  with anguish
Laidik-gaier Idler, loafer
Laks See "lox"
Lamden Scholar, erudite person, learned man
Lang leben zolt ir! Long may you live!
Langeh dronitzeh Long lean girl (Lit., a long pole)
Langer drong Lean male
Lantsman (pl., lantsleit) Countryman, neighbor, fellow
  townsman from the old country
Lapeh Big hand
Lax Smoked salmon (see Lox)
(A) Lebedikeh velt! A lively world!
(A) Lebediker Lively person
(A) Leben ahf dein kop! Words of praise like: Well
  said! Well done! (Lit., A long life upon your head.)
Lebst a chazerishen tog! Living high off the hog!
L'chei-im, le'chayim! To life! (the traditional Jewish
  toast); To your health, Down the hatch, Skol
Leibtzudekel Sleeveless shirt (like bib) with fringes,
  worn by orthodox Jews
Leiden To suffer
Lemeshkeh Caspar Milquetoast bungler

45

Leveiyeh Funeral

Lig in drerd! Get lost! Drop dead! (Lit., Bury yourself!)

Ligner Liar

Litvak Lithuanian; Often used to connote shrewdness
and also skepticism, because the Lithuanian Jews are
inclined to doubt the magic powers of the Hasidic
leaders; Also, a person who speaks with the North-
eastern Yiddish accent.

Loch Hole; vagina (taboo)

Loch in kop Hole in the head

Loi alaichem! (Hebrew) It shouldn't happen to you!
(Lit., May it not come upon you!)

Lokshen Noodles; also Italians, because they love
spaghetti! (Americanism)

Loz mich tzu ru! Leave me alone! (Lit., Let me be in
peace!)

Lox Smoked salmon (pronounced lahks)

Lishonoh tovoh tikosevu. (Hebrew) May you be inscribed for a good year (traditional greeting during the
season of the High Holy Days).

Luftmentsh Person who has no business, trade, calling,
nor income and is forced to live by improvisation, draw-
ing his livelihood "from the air" as it were (Lit., air
man); builds castles in the air; never achieves anything;
a man who starves by his wits.

Mach es kailechdik up shpitzik. Come to the point!
  (Lit., Make it round and pointy.)
Mach es shnel. Do it fast! Make it snappy! Hurry up!
Mach nit kain tsimmes fun dem! Don't make a big deal
  out of it!
Machareikeh Gimmick, contraption
Machashaifeh Witch
Machen a g'vald Make an outcry; shout for help
Machen a leben Make a living
Machen a tel fun dir. Make a nothing out of you; ruin
  you
Macher Agent with access to the authorities who pro-
  cures favors for his clients for a fee, big shot; man with
  contacts.
Macht zich nit visendik Pretends to be ignorant
(A) Magaifeh zol dich trefen! A plague on you! (Lit., A
  plague should come to you!)
Mah nishtano? (Hebrew) What is the difference? (first
  words in the opening "Four Questions" of the Passover
  Hagadah, traditionally asked by the youngest child in
  the household at the Passover Seder service)
Maidel Unmarried girl; teen-ager

Maideleh   Little girl (affectionate term)

Maivin   Expert, connoisseur, authority; sarcastically, a know-it-all who really doesn't know it all

Makeh   Plague, wound, boil, curse

Malech-hamovess   Angel of death

Malech-hamovesteh   Female angel of death; bad wife

Mamoshes   Substance; people of substance

Mamzer   Bastard (literally), disliked person, a trickster, an untrustworthy person; a superlatively clever fellow

Manyeren   Tact

Mashgiach   Inspector, overseer or supervisor of Kashruth (Jewish dietary observance) in restaurants and hotels who makes sure everything is kosher

Matriach zen   Take pains; to take the trouble; to be so good as; please

Mazel tov!   Good luck. Loads of luck. Congratulations.

Mazuma, mezuma, mezumen   Money; ready cash

Me darf nit zein shain; me darf hoben chain.   You don't have to be pretty if you have charm.

Me hot alain ungekocht.   It's your own fault (Lit., You cooked it up yourself)

Me ken brechen!   You can vomit from this!

Me ken lecken di finger!   It's delicious! (Lit., [it is so good] one can lick his fingers!)

Me ken meshugeh veren!   You can go crazy!

Me ken nit puter veren!   You can't get rid of it (him, her)!

Me ken nit tantzen ahf tsvai chassenes mit ain mol.   Take it easy. Do one thing at a time. (Lit., you can't dance at two weddings at the same time!)

Me ken tzizetst veren!   You can burst!

Me ken zich beleken!   It's delicious

Me lacht mit yashtsherklis   False or forced laugh. (Lit., Laugh with lizard's laughter)

Me lost nit leben!   They don't let you live!

Me redt, me redt un me shushkit zich.   They talk and talk and say nothing.

Me redt zich oys dos hartz!   Talk your heart out!

Me zogt   They say; it is said.

Machalel shabbes   Jew who works on or violates the Sabbath

48

Mecheieh A great pleasure; something delicious, ultra delicious, life-giving, wonderful, superb, super-joy

Mechei-ehdik Delicious tasting

Mechuten (pl., mechutonim) Relatives through marriage, In-laws. Relationship of fathers of bride and groom.

Mechutonesteh Mother of bride or groom—relationship to each other.

Megillah Scroll or the Book of Esther; in slang, it means the whole works, the complete details, a long meaningless rigamarole.

Mehlech sobyetskis yoren Good old days (Lit., the years of King Sobyetski)

Meichel Delicacy, gourmet's delight; treat

Meileh Merit, asset, advantage, virtue

Mein bobbeh's ta'am! Bad taste! Old fashioned taste! (Lit., My grandmother's taste.)

Mein cheies gait oys! I'm dying for it! (Lit., my soul expires.)

Meineh sonim zolen azoy leben! My enemies should live so!

Mekler Go-between; broker, stockbroker

Meklerkeh Female broker, go-between

Melamed (pl., melamedim) Old style orthodox Hebrew teacher in "cheder"—one room school; a wise man

Melamedkeh Wife of a melamed

Men ken es in moil nit nemen Unpalatable (Lit., You can not put it in your mouth)

Menner vash tsimmer Men's room

Menorah Traditional Jewish seven-branched candlestick; also called menoyreh

Mentsh A special man or person. This word involves a whole philosophy of life. "Mentsh" means a human being in the moral and ethical sense; not merely a person, but a person with worth and dignity, one who can be respected.

Meshugass Crazy antics; craze; madness, insanity

Meshugeh Crazy

Meshugeh ahf toit! Crazy as a loon. Really crazy! Insane (Lit., dead crazy)

Meshugeneh Mad, crazy, insane woman; an eccentric female

Meshugeneh gens, meshugeneh gribbenes Goofy parents, goofy children (Lit., crazy fowl, bad cracklings or chitterlings)

(A) Meshugeneh velt! A crazy world!

Meshugener Mad, crazy, insane man; an eccentric male

Meshugener mamzer! Crazy bastard!

Metsiyeh Bargain, a find, a favorable purchase

Meyuches Elite, cultured

Mezuma, mezumen Money; ready cash

Mezuzah Tiny box affixed to the right side of the doorway of Jewish homes containing a small portion of Deuteronomy (vi. 4-9 and xi 13-2') in twenty-two lines, handwritten on parchment.

Mich shrekt men nit! You don't frighten me! They don't frighten me! It doesn't frighten me!

Mies Ugly

Mies un mos Tedious, obnoxious

Mieskeit Ugly thing or person

Miesseh meshuneh To wish lots of trouble on someone (Lit., a strange death or a tragic end)

Miesser nefesh Cheap person

Mikveh Indoor bath or pool required for Jewish *ritual purification,* particularly during and after menstruation; A bride-to-be always goes to the mikveh before the wedding.

Milchikeh Jewish religious dietary laws distinguishes between two chief types of food: the milchikeh (dairy) and the flaishikeh (meat) which may not be eaten together; also, cutlery, dishes and utensils have to be kept separately

Milchiks All dairy foods and cutlery, dishes and cooking utensils used exclusively for dairy foods according to Jewish ritual regulations. Also pronounced Milechiks. Comes from the word "milch"—milk.

Minyan Quorum of ten men necessary for holding public worship (Young boys can also be included, provided they are over thirteen)

Mir bamien zich shtarker! We try harder!

Mir velen bentshen. We shall say grace.

Mir velen im bagroben! We'll bury him!

Mir zolen zich bagegenen ahf simches. May we meet on happy occasions.

Mirsishem (Hebrew) God willing (Contraction of Im Yirtesh Hashem)

Mirtsishem bei mir! It should happen to me, God willing!

Mishebairach (Hebrew) A blessing (Lit., He who blessed [beginning words of invoking a benediction])

Mishmash Mixture, mess, confusion, hodge podge, jumble

Mishpocheh Family, relatives

Mishpocheh-zachen Family affairs

Mittelmessiker Average man; person who is neither smart nor dumb; hoi polloi

Mitten derinnen All at once, suddenly

Mitsveh Commandment, mostly always used to mean a good deed, as helping the poor or visiting the sick; according to orthodox Jewish belief, there are 613 mitsves which Moses handed down; 365 of them were prohibitions and 248 were positive commands or mitsves.

Mizinikil Last or youngest child in family

Mizrach East; eastern; the eastern wall; front row in the synagogue, row of pews where the foremost members of the congregation sit

Mogen David David's shield, a Jewish emblem; Star of David

Mohel The religious functionary who performs circumcisions

Moid Unmarried girl; a buxom girl; an old maiden; spinster. (Usually you would say "Alteh moid"—old maid.)

Moil-shvenkechts Mouthwash

Moisheh kapoyer Mr. Upside-Down! A person who does everything wrong or in reverse

Molodyets Clever fellow; jolly good fellow

Mordeven zich To work hard

Mosser Squealer

Mumcheh Expert

Mutek Brave
Mutik heldish Brave
Mutshen zich To sweat out a job
Muttelmessig Meddlesome person, kibbitzer

N

Na! Here! (in giving) Take it. Here you are. There you
  have it
Naches Joy; Gratification, especially from children.
Nacht falt tsu. Night is falling; twilight
Nadan Dowry
Nadven (Hebrew) Philanthropist, benefactor
Nafkeh Prostitute
Nafkeh bay-is Whorehouse
Naidlechech Rare thing
Nar Fool
Nar ainer! You fool, you!
Narish Foolish
Narishkeit Foolishness
Nash Snack, sweet, treat (between meals)
Nasher A continual eater of delicacies; person with a
  sweet tooth; nibbler, especially between meals
Neb Contraction of nebbish
Nebach. It's a pity. May it not happen to you. Also a
  noun meaning an unlucky, pitiable person. A ne'er-do-
  well.
Nebbish Nobody; pitiable person, simpleton, weakling;
  shy, drab, awkward person
Nebechel Nothing, a pitiful person; or playing role of
  being one

(A) Nechtiker tog! He's (it's) gone! Forget it! Nonsense! (Lit., a yesterday's day)

Nekaiveh Female; derogatively, connotes prostitute

Nem zich a vaneh! Go take a bath! Go jump in the lake!

Neshomeh Soul, spirit; divine element in man; also refers to a child

Neshomeleh Sweetheart, darling, sweet soul (Lit., Little soul)

Nifter-shmifter, a leben macht er? What difference does it make as long as he makes a living? (Lit., nifter means deceased.)

Nishkosheh Not so bad, satisfactory. (This has nothing to do with the word "kosher," but comes from the Hebrew and means, "hard, heavy," thus "not bad." The French equivalent—pas mal.

Nisht do gedacht! It shouldn't happen! God forbid! (Lit., May we be saved from it! [sad event])

Nishtgedeiget Don't worry; doesn't worry

Nisht gefonfit! Don't hedge. Don't fool around. Don't double-talk.

Nisht geshtoigen, nisht gefloigen. It's not true whatsoever. You're not making sense! (Lit., Didn't stand, didn't fly.)

Nisht getrofen! So I guessed wrong!

Nisht gut Not good, lousy

Nisht naitik Not necessary

Nishtgutnick No-good person

Nishtikeit! A nobody!

Nishtu gedacht! It shouldn't happen! God forbid! (Lit., May we be saved from it [re: a sad event]

Nit kain farshloffener A lively person

Nit ahin, nit aher Neither here nor there.

Nit gidacht! It shouldn't happen! (Same as nishtu gedacht)

Nit gidacht gevorn. It shouldn't come to pass.

Nit kosher Impure food. Also, slang, anything not good

Nit heint, nit morgen! Not today, not tomorrow!

Nit oif undz gedacht! It shouldn't happen to us!

Nit shatten tzum shiddech. It won't hurt (him or her) in making a (nuptial) match.

Nito There is not

Nito farvos! You're welcome! (Lit., nothing to be thankful for)

—*Niu* Suffix denoting endearment

Noc hneileh! Too late! (Lit., Arriving after the closing prayers of the Day of Atonement. The last prayer on "Yom Kippur" is called "Ne-ileh," after which God has sealed the fate of a human being.)

Noch nisht Not yet

Nochshlepper Hanger-on, unwanted follower

Nor Got vaist. Only God knows.

Nu? So? Well?

Nu, shoyn! Move, already! Hurry up! Let's go! Aren't you finished? (this has infinite meanings. Lit., So, already)

Nudnik Pesty nagger, nuisance, a bore, obnoxious person

Nudje Annoying person, badgerer (Americanism)

Nudjen Badger, annoy persistently

Ober yetzt? So now? (Yetzt is also spelled itzt)
Obtshepen Get rid of
Och! Exclamation of surprise, dismay or disapproval
Och un vai! Alas and alack; woe be to it!
Oder a klop, oder a fortz (taboo) Either too much or
not enough (Lit., either a wallop or a fart)
Ohmain Amen
Oi!! Yiddish exclamation to denote disgust, pain,
astonishment or rapture
Oi, a shkandal, (oy, a skandal!) Oh, what a scandal!
Oi, gevald! Cry of anguish, suffering, frustration or for
help
Oi, vai! Dear me! Expression of dismay or hurt (Vai
means woe)
Oi vai iz mir! Woe is me!
Oisgeshtrobelt! Overdressed woman.
Oisgeshtrozelt Decorated (beautified)
Oisgetzatzket! Overdressed woman.
Ois-shteler Braggart
Oiver botel Absentminded; getting senile
Okuratner mentsh Orderly person
Oleho Hasholem (Hebrew) May she rest in peace
Olov Hasholem (Hebrew) May he rest in peace. Peace
unto him!
Olreitnik! Nouveau riche! Parvenu! (Americanism.)

On langeh hakdomes! Cut it short! (Lit., without long introductions.)

Ongeblozzen Conceited; peevish, sulky, pouting

Ongeblozzener Stuffed shirt. (Lit., Puffed up)

Ongematert Tired out

Ongepatshket Cluttered, disordered, scribbled, sloppy, littered, confusing, muddled; overly-done picture or work

Ongeshtopt Very wealthy (Lit., Stuffed up or with)

Ongeshtopt mit gelt Very wealthy; (Lit., stuffed with money)

Ongetrunken Drunk

Ongetshepter Bothersome hanger-on

Ongevarfen Cluttered, disordered

Onshikenish Hanger-on

Onshikenish Pesty nagger

Onzaltsen Giving you the business; bribe; soft-soap; sweet-talk (Lit., to salt)

Opgeflickt! Done in! Suckered! Milked! (Lit., Plucked out like a chicken)

Opgehitener Pious person

Opgekrochen Shoddy

Opgekrocheneh schoireh Shoddy merchandise

Opgelozen(er) Careless dresser

Opgenart Cheated, fooled

Opnarer Trickster, shady operator

Opnarerei Deception

Orehman Poor man, without means

Oremkeit Poverty

Oybershter God (Lit., The One above)

Oybershter in himmel God in heaven (Lit., The One above in heaven)

Oych a bashefenish Also a V.I.P.! A big person! (said derogatorily, sarcastically, or in pity)

Oych mir a leben! This too is a living! This you call living?

Oyfen himmel a yarid! Much ado about nothing! Impossible! (Lit., In heaven there's a big fair!)

Oyfgekumener Come upper, upstart

Oyfgekumener g'vir Parvenu, nouveau riche

Oys shiddech.   The marriage is off!
Oysgedart Skinny, emaciated
Oysgehorevet Exhausted
Oysgematert Tired out, worn out
Oysgemutshet Worked to death, tired out
Oysgeputst Dressed up, overdressed; overdecorated
Oysgetsert Emaciated
Oysvurf Outcast, bad person
Oyver butel Senile, absent-minded, mixed up

Paigeren zol er!   He should drop dead!

Pamelech   Slow, slowly

Parech   Low-life, a bad man (Lit., having scabs on head)

Parechavatter   Low-life, bad man

Parnosseh   Livelihood

Parshiveh   Mean, cheap

Parshoin   He-man

Partatshnek   Inferior merchandise or work

Parveh   Neutral food, neither milchidik (dairy) nor flaishidik (meat)

Paskudnik, paskudnyak   Ugly, revolting, disgusting fellow; mean, evil person; nasty fellow; punk

Past nit.   It isn't proper.

Patsh   Slap, smack on the cheek

Patsher.   A person who carries on work or sport in a slipshod, unbusinesslike, half-assed manner.

Patshken   Mess around, to soldier on job, to work or play half-heartedly; futz around, doing things in a time-wasting manner without adequate results

Patshkies around   Anglicized characterization of one engaged in patshken

Patteren tseit   To lounge around; waste time

Pavolyeh   Slow, slowly

Peeric (taboo) Vagina

Petseleh Little penis (affectionately applied to infant boy)

Phooey! fooey, pfui Designates disbelief, distaste, contempt

Pipek. Navel, belly button, gizzard; same as "pupik"

Pirgeh (taboo) Vagina

Pishechtz (taboo) Urine

Pishen (taboo) Urinate, piss

Pisher (taboo) Male infant; a nobody; a little squirt. (Lit., a urinator)

Pisherkeh (taboo) Female infant (affectionate term); a nobody! (derogative term when applied to adult females; Lit., little urinator)

Pishteppel Pee pot

Pisk Slang, for mouth (moyl); insultingly, it means big mouth, loudmouth; a mouthpiece.

Pisk-Malocheh Big talker—little doer! (man who talks a good line but accomplishes nothing; Lit., work by mouth)

Pitshetsh Coquette, chronic complainer

Pitsel Wee, tiny

Pitsvinik Little nothing

Plagen Work hard, sweat out a job, suffer

Plagen zich To suffer

Plaplen Chatter

Plats! Burst! Bust your guts out! Split your guts!

Platsen To burst, bust

Plyotkenitzeh A gossip

Pooh! Exclamation of disdain

Potz (taboo) Penis (insulting when you call a man that)

Poyer Peasant, rustic, farmer, boor, dullard

Preplen To mutter, mumble

Preitzteh Princess; finicky girl; (having airs, giving airs; being snooty) prima donna!

Prost Coarse, common, vulgar

Prostaches Low class people

Prostak Ignorant boor, coarse person, vulgar man

Prosteh leit Simple people, common people; vulgar, ignorant, "low class" people

Proster mentsh Vulgar man, common man

Proster oilem Common people

Pupik Navel, belly button, gizzard, chicken stomach; (also a term of teasing endearment)

Pupiklech Dish of chicken gizzards

Pushkeh Poor box (in every traditional Jewish home, odd coins are put in this, particularly on Friday afternoon, before the Sabbath begins; money is used for the support of philanthropic and educational institutions)

Pustunpasnik Loafer, idler

Putskeh Something decorative, from "putsen," to decorate.

Pyesseh A play, drama

R

Rachmones   Compassions, mercy, pity

Rav   Rabbi, religious leader of the community

Reb   Mr., Rabbi; title given to a learned and respected man

Rebiniu   "Rabbi dear!" Term of endearment for a rabbi

Rebitsin   Literally, the rabbi's wife (often sarcastically appied to a woman who gives herself airs, or acts excessively pious); pompous woman

Rechielesnitseh   Dowdy, gossipy woman

Reden on a moss   To chatter without end

Redn tzu der vant   Talk in vain or to talk and receive no answer (Lit., talk to the wall for all the good it will do you)

Redt zich ein a krenk!   Imaginary sickness

Reich   Rich, wealthy

Reisen di hoit   Skin someone alive (Lit., to tear the skin)

Ribi-fish, gelt oyfen tish!   Don't ask for credit! Pay in cash in advance! Cash on the barrel-head! Money on the table!

Riboynoy-shel-oylom! (Hebrew)   God in heaven, Master of the Universe.

Richtiker chaifetz   The real article! The real McCoy!

Rirevdiker   A lively person

Rolleh   Acting a role in a play

Rosheh   Mean, evil person

(A) Ruach in dein taten's taten arein!   Go to the devil (Lit., A devil [curse] should enter your father's father!)

Ruf mich k'nak-nissel!   I did wrong? So call me a nut!

Ruktish   Portable table

Saichel   Common sense, good sense; tact, diplomacy

Sara . . . !   What a . . . ! What kind of a . . . !

S'art eich?   What does it matter to you? Does it matter to you?

S'art mich vi di vant!   I don't give a care!

Se brent nit!   Don't get excited! (Lit., It's not on fire!)

Se hert zich a raiech!   It stinks! It gives off a bad odor.

Se shtinkt!   It stinks!

Se tsegait zich in moyl!   Yummy-yummy! (It melts in your mouth!)

Se zol dir grihmen in boych!   You should get a stomach cramp!

Sha!   (gently said) Please keep quiet (shouted) Quiet! Shut up!

Shabbes goy   Someone doing the dirty work for others (Lit., gentile doing work for a Jew on Sabbath)

Shadchen   Matchmaker or marriage broker; (There is the professional type who derives his living from it, but many Jewish women used to engage in matchmaking without compensation only from religious motives)

Shaigetz   Non-Jewish boy; wild Jewish boy

Shaigetz ainer! Berating term for irreligious Jewish boy, especially one who blatantly flouts Jewish law; fellow of great audacity

Shain vi di zibben velten Beautiful as the seven worlds

Shaineh literatur Belles lettres

Shaineh maidel Pretty girl

Shainer gelechter Hearty laugh (sarcastically, Some laughter!)

Shainkeit Beauty

Shaitel, (sheitel) Wig (at the wedding the ultra-orthodox bride has her hair cut off and she wears a shaitel ever after)

Shalach mohnes Customary gifts exchanged on Purim, usually goodies

Shalom Peace (a watchword and a greeting) Shalom Alaichem—peace unto you; hello; also, Good-bye, So long; also spelled sholom

Shammes Sexton, beadle of the synagogue, also, the lighter taper used to light other candles on a menorah, a policeman (slang)

Shandhoiz Brothel, whorehouse

Shat, shat! Hust! Quiet! Don't get excited!

Shatnes Proscription against wearing clothes that are mixed of wool and linen

Shema (Hebrew) Hear Ye! (the first word in the confession of the Jewish faith: "Hear O Israel: the Lord our God, the Lord is One!" It consists of the following passages: Deut. 6:4-9; 11:13-21 and Num. 5:37-41

Shemen zich in dein veiten haldz! You ought to be ashamed of yourself (Lit., You should be ashamed down to the bottom of your throat)

Shemevdik Bashful, shy

Shenereh laigt men in drerd. Prettier ones they bury! (implying the girl is ugly)

Shepen naches Enjoy; gather pleasure, draw pleasure, especially from children

Shidech (pl., shiduchim) Match, marriage, betrothal.

Shihi-pihi Mere nothings

Shik-yingel Messenger

Shikker Drunkard

Shikseh Non-Jewish girl (also used to imply an impious or wild Jewish girl)

Shinden di hoit Skin someone

Shiva Mourning period of seven days observed by family and friends of deceased

Shkapeh. A hag, a mare; worthless

Shkotz Berating term for mischievous Jewish boy

Shlak Apoplexy; a wretch, a miserable person; shoddy; shoddy merchandise

Shlak joint Store that sells cheap, inferior merchandise, second-hand or cut-rate goods, where bargaining over prices is important (Americanism)

Shlang Snake, serpent; a troublesome wife; penis (taboo)

Shlanger (taboo) Long or big penis

Shlatten shammes Communal busybody, tale bearer; messenger

Shlecht Bad

Shlecht veib Shrew (Lit., a bad wife)

Shlemiel Clumsy bungler, an inept person, butter-fingered; dopey person, fool, simpleton

Shlep Drag, carry or haul, particularly unnecessary things, parcels or baggage; to go somewhere unwillingly or unwantedly

Shleppen To drag, pull, carry, haul

Shlepper Sponger, panhandler, hanger-on; dowdy, gossipy woman; stupid person, dolt; a free-loader, one who expects something for nothing

Shlimazel Luckless person. Unlucky person; incompetent person; one who has perpetual bad luck (Everything bad happens to him; it is said that the shlemiel spills the soup on the shlimazel!)

Shlog zich kop in vant. Go break your own head! (Lit., bang your head against the wall)

Shlog zich mit Got arum! Go fight City Hall! (Lit., Go fight with God.)

Shlogen To beat up

Shlok A curse; apoplexy

Shlosser Mechanic

Shlub A jerk; a foolish, stupid or unknowing person, same as shlump; second rate, inferior.

Shlump　Careless dresser, untidy person, foolish, dumb
　　person; a jerk; as a verb, to idle or lounge around
Shlumper　Same as shlump
Shlumperdik　Unkempt, sloppy
Shlumpf　Sucker, patsy, fall guy, second rater
Shlumpy　Sweaty, unkempt
Shmaltz　Grease or fat; (slang) flattery; to sweet talk,
　　overly praise; gooey (food)
Shmaltzy　Sentimental, corny
Shmatteh　Rag, anything worthless
Shmeis　Bang, wallop
Shmek　A smell
Shmek tabik　Nothing of value (Lit., a pinch of snuff)
Shmeer　The business; the whole works; to bribe, to coat
　　like butter, to be excessively kind for selfish gain
Shmegegi　Buffoon, idiot, fool. See shmendrik
Shmeichel　To butter up
Shmeikel　To swindle, con, fast-talk.
Shmendrik　Fool; nincompoop; an inept or indifferent
　　person (or one to whom you are indifferent); a dope,
　　shlemiel, simpleton
Shmirt zich oys di shich!　You're welcome (in my home)
　　(Lit., Wipe your shoes clean)
Shmo(e)　Naive person, easy to deceive; a goof
　　(Americanism)
Shmock (taboo)　Self-made fool; obscene for penis;
　　derisive term for a man
Shmohawk　Anglicized variant for "shmock" (penis)
Shmontses　Trifles, folly
Shmooz; (shmuess)　Chat, talk
Shmoozen, (shmuessen)　To discuss or converse idly or
　　pleasantly
Shmulky!　A sad sack!
Shmuts　Dirt, slime
Shmutzik　Dirty, soiled
Shnapps　Whiskey, same as bronfen
Shnecken　Little fruit and nut coffee rolls
Shneider　Tailor; in gin rummy card game, to win game
　　without opponent scoring
Shnell　Quick, quickly
Shnook　A patsy, a dolt, a sucker, a sap, a meek person

easy to impose on; Casper Milquetoast; easy-going, gullible

Shnorrer A beggar who makes pretensions to respectability; sponger, chiseler, moocher; a parasite, but always with brass and resourcefulness in getting money from others as though it were his right

Shnur Daughter-in-law

Schochet A ritual slaughterer of animals and fowl

Sholem alaichem Hebrew-Yiddish salutation, Peace be to you (The person greeted responds in reverse, Alaichem sholem, To you be peace. Equivalent to hello. How are you? How do you do? Good-bye)

Shoymer Watchman; historically refers also to the armed Jewish watchman in the early agricultural settlements in the Holy Land

Shoymet mitzves Pious person

Shoyn ainmol a' metsei-eh! Really a bargain

Shoyn fargessen? You have already forgotten?

Shoyn genug! That's enough!

Shoyn opgetrent? (taboo) Have you finished the dirty work? (Lit., Have you finished fornicating?)

Shpilkes Pins and needles

Shpitsfinger Toes

Shpitz bekitzur! Cut it short!

Shpogel nei Brand-new

Shreklecheh zach A terrible thing

Shprichvort (pl., shprichverter) Proverb, saying

Shtain reich Very rich (Lit., Stone rich)

Shtark, shtarker Strong, brave

Shtark gehert Smelled bad (used only in reference to food; Lit., strongly heard)

Shtark vi a ferd Strong as a horse

(A) Shtarker Tough guy, a roughneck, a strong-arm character; a bully

(A) Shtarker charakter A strong character

Shav Cold spinach soup, sorrel grass soup, sour leaves soup

Shtik Piece, bit, lump; a special bit of acting

Shtik drek (taboo) Piece of shit; shit-head

Shtik goy Idiomatic expression for one inclined to

heretical views, or to ignorance of Jewish religious values

Shtik holtz Dumb like a piece of wood (Lit., Piece of wood)

Shtik naches Grandchild, child, or relative who gives you pleasure or satisfaction; a great joy (Lit., A piece of pleasure)

Shtik nar A big fool! Some fool!

Shtikel Small bit or piece; a morsel

Shtiklech Tricks; small pieces

Shtilinkerait Quietly

Shtinken To stink

Shtoltz Pride; unreasonably and stubbornly proud, excessive self-esteem

Strudel Sweet cake made of paper-thin dough rolled up with various fillings—usually fruit and nuts—and baked

(A) Shtunk A guy who doesn't smell too good, also applicable to a female; a stink (bad odor); a lousy human

Shtup Push, shove; vulgarism for sexual intercourse (taboo)

Shtup es in toches! (taboo) Shove (or stick) it up your rectum!

Shul Colloquial Yiddish for synagogue; said to have stemmed from Germans who, seeing Jews studying in the synagogue, mistook the synagogue for a shul or school; according to another opinion, from the Latin term, a schola', used by Italian Jews as meaning community

Shule School

Shush! Quiet!

Shushkeh A whisper; an aside

Shushken zich To whisper, to gossip

Shutfim Associates

Shvachkeit Weakness

(A) Shvartz yor! A black year!

Shvebeleh Highly excitable person. (Lit., a match)

Shvegerin Sister-in-law

Shveig! Quiet! Stop talking!

Shvengern Be pregnant

Shver   Father-in-law; heavy, hard, difficult
Shver tsu machen a leben   It's tough to make a living!
Shviger   Mother-in-law
Shvindel   Fraud, deception, swindle
Shvindeldik   Dizzy, unsteady
Shvindilt in di oygen   Blinding the eyes; feeling dizzy
Shvitser   "A big producer" (who doesn't produce); a braggart
Shvitz bod   Steam bath
Shvoger   Brother-in-law
Shvontz (taboo)   Man who behaves stupidly, ungallantly, obscenely, or idiotically (Lit., tail); penis (uncomplimentary)
Sidder   Jewish prayer book for weekdays and Saturday
Simcheh   Joy; also refers to a joyous occasion, such as a birth, bar-mitzvah, engagement, marriage, etc.
Sitzfleish   Patience that can endure sitting (Lit., sitting flesh)
S'iz mir gut!   It's great!
S'iz oys.   It's over. It's gone!
Skotzel kumt   A caustic greeting used principally in reference to women
S'macht nit oys.   It doesn't matter.
Smetteneh   Sour cream; Cream
Sof kol sof   Finally
S'teitsh!   Listen! Hold on! How is that? How is that possible? How come?
Strasheh mich nit!   Don't threaten me!
Szhlob   Moron
Szhlok   Nincompoop; ne'er-do-well

T.O.T. (See Toches ahfen tish)

Ta'am Taste, flavor; good taste

Tahkeh Really! Is that so? Certainly!

Tahkeh a metsieh Really a bargain! (usually said with sarcasm)

Taiglech Small pieces of baked dough or little cakes dipped in honey

Tallis Rectangular prayer-shawl to whose four corners fringes (tzitzis) are attached (used by male Jews during morning prayers)

Talis koten Religious fringed garment

Talmud The complete treasury of Jewish law interpreting the Torah (Five Books of Moses) into livable law

Talmud Torah The commandment to study the Law; an educational institution for orphans and poor children, supported by the community; in the United States, a Hebrew school for children

Tamavateh Naive, simple-minded, feeble-minded

Tandaitneh Inferior

Tararam Big noise, big deal

Tashlich Ceremony of the casting off of sins on the Jewish New Year (crumbs of bread symbolizing one's sins are cast away into a stream of water in the afternoon of the Jewish New Year, Rosh Hashoneh

Tateh, tatteh, tatteleh, tatinka, tatteniu Father, papa, daddy, pop

Tateh-mameh, papa-mama Parents

Tateniu Father dear (The suffix "niu" in Yiddish is added for endearing intimacy; also, God is addressed this way by the pious; Tateniu-Foter means God, our Father

Tefillin (Phylacteries) (Leather cubes containing scriptual texts inscribed on parchment; they are a sign of the covenant between God and Israel. They are worn by males over thirteen years old; see Bar-mitzvah)

Teier Dear, costly, expensive

Tei-yerinkeh! Sweetheart, dearest

Telerel fun himel Something unattainable; the moon on a plate (Lit., A plate from heaven)

Temp Dolt

Temper kop Dullard

Tinif Worthless! (Lit., excreta)

T'noim Bethrothal, engagement

Toches Buttocks, behind, fanny

Toches ahfen tish! (taboo) Put up or shut up! Let's conclude this! Come clean, buddy! (Lit., Buttocks on the table!)

Toches-lecker (taboo) Person who will do anything to gain favor; brown-noser, apple-polisher, ass-kisser (Lit., Buttock-licker)

Togshul Day school

Tog-teglech Day-to-day, daily

Toig ahf kapores! Good for nothing! It's worth nothing!

Toit hungerik Starved, dead hungry

Tokus, (tokis, tuckus) (taboo) Posterior, rectum, buttocks, ass, behind (variant of "toches")

Toonked (tunked) Dunked, dipped

Traif Forbidden food, impure, contrary to the Jewish dietary laws, or not prepared according to regulations (applied also to forbidden literature and other non-kosher matters)

Traifener bain Jew who does not abide by Jewish law (derisive, scornful expression; Lit., non-kosher bone)

Traifeneh bicher Forbidden literature

72

Traifnyak Despicable person; one who eats non-kosher food

Tranteh Rag; (used sarcastically) decrepit, useless, worn out

Tren zich (taboo) Frig you! Go fornicate yourself!

Trenen To tear, rip, rape

Tripper Gonorrhea

Trogedik Pregnant

Trog gezunterhait! Wear it in good health!

Trombenik A bum, no-good person, ne'er-do-well; a faker

Tsaddik Pious, righteous person

Tsap mir nit mein blut! Don't bleed me!

Tsatskeh Doll, plaything; something cute (like a girl); an overdressed woman; a sexually attractive girl

Tsatskeleh der mamehs! Mother's favorite! Mother's pet!

Tsebrech a fus! Break a leg!

Tsedokeh Spirit of philanthropy; charity, benevolence

Tsedrait Nutty, crazy, screwy

Tsedraiter kop Bungler

Tsedrumshket Confused

Tsedrumshki Befuddled

Tsekocht Excited

Tsemisht Confused, befuddled, mixed-up

Tshatshki Toy, doo-dad; pretty girl (see tsatskeh)

Tshav Cold spinach soup, sorrel grass soup, sour leaves soup (usually pronounced "shav")

Tshepeh zich nit tsu mir! Don't bother me! (Lit., Don't attach yourself to me!)

Tshepeh zich op fun mir! Get away from me! Leave me alone!

Tshepen To annoy, irk, plague, bother, attack unwantedly

Tsevishen-shtotisheh telefonistkeh Long distance operator

Tsegait zich in moyl It melts in the mouth, delicious, yummy-yummy

Tsemishnich Confusion

Tsetrogen Absent-minded

73

Tsevildeter   Wild person

Tsiklen zich   The cantor's ecstatic repetition of a musical phrase

Tsimmes   Sweet carrot compote; (slang) a major issue made out of a minor event; a fuss over nothing

Tsitskeh   Breast, teat, udder

Tsnueh   Chaste

Tsores   Troubles, misery

Tsu kumen oifen zinen   To come to mind

Tsu shand un tsu shpot   In disgrace and humiliation

Tsutsheppenish   Hanger-on; unwanted companion; pest nuisance

Tsum glik, tsum shlimazel   For better, for worse

Tu mir a toiveh.   Do me a favor.

Tu mir nit kain toives.   Don't do me any favors.

Tu mir tsulib.   Do me a favor. Do it for my sake.

Tuckus   (See Toches)

Tumel   Confusion, noise, uproar

Tumler   A noise-maker (person); an agitator, boisterer roisterer

Tush   Buttock (refers only to an infant's)

Tut mir hanoeh   It gives me pleasure (also used sarcastically)

Tut vai dos harts   Heartbroken

Tzatzkeh   Ornament, toy; a dingus, doo-dad; a living doll, a sexually attractive girl; an overdressed woman; a playgirl (same as "tsatskeh")

Tzitzis   Fringes attached to the four corners of the tallis, the prayer shawl

Tzufil!   Too much! Too dear! Too costly!

Tzu tei-er   Too costly

Tzures   Troubles (same as tsores)

Um-be-rufen Unqualified, uncalled for; God forbid; (A
deprecation to ward off evil)

Um-be-shrien God forbid! It shouldn't happen! (A
deprecation to ward off evil)

Umgeduldik Petulant

Ummeglick! Impossible!

Umglick A misfortune, tragedy; when it refers to a man,
it means a born loser; an unlucky one

Umshteller Braggart

Umzist For nothing

Un langeh hakdomes! Cut it short! (Lit., Without a long
introduction)

Unterkoifen To bribe

Untershmeichlen To butter up

Untervelt mentsh Racketeer

Utz To goad, to needle

Vai! Woe, pain; usually appears as "oi vai!"

Vai iz mir! Woe is me!

Vais ich vos Stuff and nonsense! So you say! (Lit., Know from what)

Vaitik An ache

Valgeren zich Wander around aimlessly

Valgerer Homeless wanderer

Vaneh Bath, bathtub, tub

Vantz Bedbug; (slang) a nobody

Varenikehs Pastry made of rounds of noodle dough filled with jelly, fruit, or meat, and fried

Varfen an oyg To watch out; to guard; to mind; (Lit., To throw an eye at)

Varnishkes Kasha with noodles; stuffed potato cakes

Vart! Wait! Hold on!

Vash-tsimmer Bathroom, washroom

Vash-tsimmer far froyen Ladies' room

Vash-tsimmer far menner Men's room

Vechter Watchman

Veibernik Debauchee

Veibersheh shtik Female tricks

Veis vi kalech! Pale as a sheet!

Vek-zaiger Alarm clock

Vemen barestu? (taboo)   Whom are you kidding? Whom are you fooling? (Lit., Whom are you screwing?)

Vemen narstu?   Whom are you fooling?

Ven ich ess, hob ich zai alleh in drerd   When I eat, they can all go to hell!

Ver derharget!   Get killed! Drop dead! (Also "ver geharget")

Ver dershtikt!   Choke yourself!

Ver farblondjet!   Get lost! Go away!

Ver vaist?   Who knows?

Ver volt dos geglaibt?   Who would have believed it?

Veren a tel   To be ruined

Vi a barg   Large as a mountain

Vi der ruach zogt gut morgen   Where the devil says good morning! (had many meanings; usually appended to another phrase)

Vi gàit dos gesheft?   How's business?

Vi gait es eich?   How goes it with you?

Vi gaits?   How goes it? How are things? How's tricks?

Vi haistu?   What's your name?

Vi ruft men . . . ?   What is the name of . . . ?

Vi ruft men eich?   What is your name?

Viazoy?   How come?

Vifil?   How much?

Vilder mentsh   A wild one; a wild person

Vilstu . . .   Do you want . . .

Voglen   To wander around aimlessly

Voiler yung!   Roughneck (sarcastic expression)

Vo den?   What else?

Vortshpiel   Pun, witticism

Vos art es (mich)?   What does it matter (to me)? What do I care?

Vos barist du? (taboo)   What are you screwing around for? What are you fooling around for?

Vos bei a nichteren oyfen lung, is bei a shikkeren oyfen tsung.   What a sober man has on his lung (mind), a drunk has on his tongue.

Vos draistu mir a kop?   What are you bothering me for? (Lit., Why are you twisting my head?)

Vos failt zai?   What are they lacking?

Vos gicher, alts besser   The faster, the better

Vos hakst du mir in kop?   What are you talking my head off for?

Vos hert zich?   What do you hear around? What's up?

Vos hert zich epes nei-es?   What's new?

Vos hob ich dos gedarft?   What did I need it for?

Vos-in-der-kort   Capable of doing anything bad (applied to bad person; Lit., everything in the cards)

Vos iz?   What's the matter?

Vos iz ahfen kop, iz ahfen tsung!   What's on his mind is on his tongue!

Vos iz der chil'lek?   What difference does it make?

Vos iz der tachlis?   What's the purpose? Where does it lead to?

Vos iz di chochmeh?   What is the trick?

Vos iz di untershteh shureh?   What's the point? What's the outcome? (Lit., What's on the bottom line?)

Vos iz mit dir?   What's wrong with you?

Vos kocht zich in teppel?   What's cooking?

Vos macht dos oys?   What difference does it make?

Vos macht es mir oys?   What difference does it make to me?

Vos macht ir?   How are you? (pl.); How do you do?

Vos machstu?   How are you? (sing.)

Vos maint es?   What does it mean?

Vos noch?   What else? What then?

Vos ret ir epes?   What are you talking about?

Vos tut zich?   What's going on? What's cooking?

Vos vet zein (Que sera?)   What will be?

Vos vet zein, vet zein!   What will be, will be!

Vos zogt ir?   What are you saying?

Vu tut dir vai?   Where does it hurt you?

Vuhin gaistu?   Where are you going?

Vund   Wound

Vursht   Bologna

Vyzoso   Idiot (named after youngest son of Haman, archenemy of Jews in Book of Esther); also, penis

78

Yachneh A course, loud-mouthed woman; a gossip; a slattern

Yachsen Man of distinguished lineage, highly connected person; privileged character

Yarmelkeh Traditional Jewish skull cap, worn usually during prayers; worn at all times by observant Orthodox Jews, to indicate that someone (God) is above them; also worn by Catholic prelates

Yatebedam A man who threatens; one who thinks he's a big shot; a blusterer

Yeder mentsh hot zeineh aigeneh meshugahss. Every person has his own idiosyncrasies.

Yedies News; cablegrams; announcements

Yefayfiyeh Beauty; woman of great beauty

Yenems Someone else's; the other's (the brand of cigarettes moochers smoke!)

Yeneh velt The other world; the world to come

Yenteh Gaggy, talkative woman; female blabbermouth

Yentzen (taboo) To fornicate, to whore

Yentzer (taboo) Fornicator, whoremaster

Yeshiveh Jewish traditional higher school, talmudical academy

Yeshiveh bocher Student of talmudic academy

Yeshuvnik Farmer, rustic

Yichus Pedigree, ancestry, family background, nobility

Yiddisher kop Jewish head

Yingeh tsats-keh! A young doll! A living doll!

Yisgadal, vyiskadash (Hebrew) First two words of mourner's prayer honoring the dead

Yiskor Prayer in commemoration of the dead (Lit., May God remember.)

Yold! Dope, boor, chump, hick

Yontefdik Festive, holiday-ish; sharp (referring to clothes)

Yontiff Any Jewish holiday (also spelled yomtov and yontev from the Hebrew—"yom tov"—a good day.)

Yortseit Anniversary of the day of death of parents or other relatives; yearly remembrance of the dead

Yoysher Justice, fairness, integrity

Yukel Buffoon

(A) Yung mit bainer! A powerhouse! Strongly built person (Lit., A boy with sturdy bones)

Yung un alt Young and old

Yungatsh Street-urchin, scamp, young rogue

Yungermantshik A young, vigorous lad; a newlywed

Zaft Juice

Zaftik Pleasantly plump and pretty (woman); well-stacked; sensuous looking (Lit., juicy)

Zaftikeh moid! Sexually attractive girl

Zaideh Grandfather

Zaier gut O.K. (Lit., very good)

Zaier shain gezogt! Well said! (Lit., Very beautifully said!)

Zeh nor, zeh nor! Look here, look here!

Zei (t) gezunt Be well! Good-bye! Farewell

Zei mir frailich! Be happy!

Zei mir gezunt! Be well!

Zei mir matriach Be at pains to . . . Please; make an effort.

Zei nit a nar! Don't be a fool!

Zei nit kain goylem! Don't be a fool! Don't be a robot!

Zei nit kain vyzoso! Don't be a damn fool! Don't be an idiot! also, don't be a penis! (taboo)

Zeit azoy gut Please (Lit., Be so good)

Zeit ir doch ahfen ferd! You're all set! (Lit., You're on the horse!)

Zeit (mir) moychel Excuse me! Be so good as . . . Forgive me!

81

Zelig Blessed (used mostly among German Jews in recalling a beloved deceased—mama zelig)

Zeltenkeit Rare thing

Zetz Punch, bang! Pow! Also slang for a sexual experience (taboo)

Zhaleven To be sparing, miserly

Zhlob A jerk; foolish, stupid, uncouth

Zhulik Faker

Zhumerei Whirring noise

Zhumet Makes a whirring noise

Zif armacht nit dos moyl She doesn't stop talking (Lit., She doesn't close her mouth)

Zindik nit Don't complain. Don't sin. Don't tempt the Gods.

Ziseh neshomeh Sweet soul

Ziseh raidelech Sweet talk

Ziskeit Sweet thing, sweetness (also endearing term for child)

Zitsen ahf shpilkes Sitting on pins and needles; being fidgety

Zitzen shiveh Sit in mourning (Shiveh means seven, the number of days in the mourning period)

Zitsflaish Patience (Lit., Sitting meat)

Zog a por verter! Say a few words!

Zogen a ligen Tell a lie.

Zogerkeh Woman who leads the prayers in the women's section in the synagogue

Zoineh Prostitute

Zol dich chapen beim boych. You should get a stomach cramp!

Zol dir klappen in kop! It should bang in your head (as it's annoying me!)

Zol er tsebrechen a fus! May he break a leg! He should break a leg!

Zol es brennen! The hell with it. (Lit., let it burn!)

Zol Got mir helfen! May God help me!

Zol Got ophiten! May God prevent!

Zol ich azoy vissen fun tsores! I haven't got the faintest idea! (Lit., I should so know from trouble as I know about this!)

Zol vaksen tzibbelis fun pipek! Onions should grow from your navel!

Zol zein! Let it be! That's it!

Zol zein azoy! O.K.! Let it be so!

Zol zein gezunt! Be well! It (you, etc.) should be well!

Zol zein mit glik! Good luck!

Zol zein shah! Be quiet!

Zol zein shtil! Silence! Be quiet! Let's have some quiet!

Zolstu azoy laiben! You should live so!

Zolst geshvollen veren vi a barg! You should swell up like a mountain!

Zolst leben un zein gezunt! You should live and be well!

Zolst ligen in drerd! Drop dead! (Lit., You should lie in the earth!)

Zolst nit vissen fun kain shlechts. You shouldn't know from bad (evil).

Zolst es shtipin in toches! (taboo) Shove it up your (anus) rectum!

Zorg zich nit! Don't worry!

Zshlob · Slob

Zuninkeh! Dear son! Darling son!

ENGLISH-YIDDISH

ABC's Alef-bais

A.K. Alter Kucker (taboo)

A bad person (capable of doing anything bad or evil!) Vos-in-der-kort

A big, good-for-nothing A groisser gornisht

A big, healthy dame A gezunteh moid

A blessing Mi shebairach (sarcastically means a curse)

A blessing on your head A leben ahf dein kop; a brocheh ahf dein kop (used to mean "Well said!" "Well done!")

A curse on my enemies A klog tzu meineh sonim

A curse on you! A broch tsu dir! A choleryeh ahf dir! A finster yor ahf dir!

A fool feels nothing A nar filt nit

A great joy A shtik naches

A Hebrew school Talmud Torah

A little A bisel

A little nothing Shmendrik, nishtikeit, gornit

A lot to tell, little to hear A sach tsu reden, vainik tsu herren

A lucky thing happened to you! A glick hot dich getrofen!

A one and only An ain un aintsikeh

84

A person who drops whatever he touches   Gelaimter

A pig remains a pig   A chazer bleibt a chazer

A plague!   A magaifeh! A finsternish!

A plague on you!   A choleryeh ahf dir!

A shame and disgrace   A shandeh un a charpeh

A smell and a taste (what you get when a hostess serves peanut-size hors d'oeuvres—and too few of them)   A lek un a shmek

A strong character   A shtarker charakter

Absent-minded   Tsetrogen; oiver botel

Absolutely nothing!   Kadoches mit koshereh fodem!

Accursed   Geshtroft

(An) Ache   Vaitik

Acting bit   Shtik

Advantage   Meileh

Agent with access to the authorities who procures favors for his clients for a fee   Macher

Agitator   Tumler (at a resort)

Alarm clock   Vek-zaiger

Alas and alack!   Och un vai!

All at once   Mitten derinnen

All shoemakers go barefoot.   Aleh shusters gaien borves.

Alphabet   Alef-bais (the first two letters of the Hebrew-Yiddish alphabet)

Also a V.I.P.!   Oych a bashefenish!

Amen   Ohmain

Ancestry   Yichus

Anecdote   Meiseleh

Angel of death (male)   Malech-hamovess (sarcastically, bad husband)

(female)   Malech-hamovesteh (sarcastically, bad wife)

Angry (with)   Kaas (in kaas oyt), baroygis

Angry person   Kaasnick, kaasen, farbrenter

Animal (cow)   Behaimeh (when referring to human being, means dull-witted)

Animal (wild)   Chei-eh, vildeh chei-eh

Anniversary of the death of a person   Yortseit

Announcements   Yedies

(To) Annoy   Tshepen zich, tsutshepen

85

Annoy persistently Nudjen, tshepen zich

Annoying person Nudje, nudnik

Another man's disease is not hard to endure. A makeh unter yenems orem iz nit shver tzu trogen.

Antique Tranteh (refers to rag; sarcastically, worn out or useless)

Any Jewish holiday Yontiff, also spelled yomtov and yontev

Anybody no good at their job Kalyekeh

Anything bad to eat or own Chazzerei

Anything worthless Shmatteh (Lit., rag)

Anxious Fardeiget

Apoplexy Shlak

Appetizer Forshpeiz

Apple-polisher Toches-lecker (taboo)

Are you beginning again? Fangst shoin on? Haibst shoin on?

Are you crazy? Bistu meshugeh?

Are you in a hurry? Bist ahf ain fus?

Are you starting up again? Du fangst shoyn on?

Aren't you finished? Nu, shoyn?

Artisan Balmelocheh

As futile as stomping on the earth Es iz vert a zets in drerd

As long as I can be with you Abi tsu zein mit dir

As long as you're healthy Abi gezunt

As unimportant as dung on a piece of wood Drek ahf a shpendel (taboo)

(An) Aside Shushkeh

Ass Chamoyer, ezel, eizel; Freg mich becherim

Asset Meileh

Ass-licker (taboo) Toches-lecker

Ass-kisser (taboo) Toches-lecker

Associates Chevreh, chaverim, shutfim

Assuredly Tahkeh

Astonishment (exclamation) Oi!

Atonement Kaporeh

Attractive girl Tsatskeh

(An) Authority Maivin

Average man Mittelmessiker
Aw, hell! A broch!
Awful! Geferlech!
Awkward person Klotz, kunyehlemmel; nebbish, nebach

B

Baby son Kaddishel (endearing term)
Bachelor, unmarried man Bocher, nit baveibter, alter bocher
Back-handed slap Frassk
Backside Hinten
Bad Shlecht, kalyeh
Bad odor Ippish
(A) Bad man Parech, parechavatter, oisvurf
Bad person Oisvurf, vos-in-der-kort
Bad taste Main bobbeh's ta'am (Lit., My grandmother's taste)
(To) Badger Nudjen
(A) Badgerer Nudje, nudnik
(A mere) Bagatelle Bubkes, bobkes; ain klainikeit!
Baked dumplings (filled with potato, meat, liver or barley) K'nishes (pronounce the K!)
(A) Bang Chmalyeh, klop, zetz, k'nack
Bang your head against the wall! Klop zich kop in vant!
Barefoot Borves
Barely able to creep Kam vos er kricht
Barely alive! Kam vos er lebt!
Barely made it! Kam mit tsores!
Bargain Metsieh

(To) Bargain Dingen zich, handlen
Bashful Shemevdik
Bastard Mamzer
Bath Vaneh, bod
Bath-ritual Mikveh
Be at pains to, (please) Zeit zich matriach
Be happy! Zeit frailich!
Be so good, (please) Zeit azoy gut!
Be so good as Zeit moychel; zeit zich matriach
Be quiet! Zol zein shtil! Zol zein sha!
(To) Be ruined Veren a tel
Be well! Zei(t) gezunt
Beadle of the synagogue Shammes
(To) Beam Kvelen
(To) Beam with delight and pride K'velen fun naches
Beans Bubkes, beblech
Beast Behaimeh; (sarcastically, fool)
Beat it! Chap a gang! Farnem zich fun danen! Gai avek!
(To) Beat up Shlogen
Beautiful as the seven worlds Shain vi di zibben velten
Beautiful woman Krassavitseh
(A) Beauty Krassavitseh, shainkeit, yefayfiyeh
Bedbug Vantz
Beet soup Borsht
Befuddled Farmisht, tsemisht, tsedrumshki, tsetumelt, fartshadikt
Beggar Shnorrer, hoizer, gaier, betler
Behind (buttocks) Toches, inten, hinten
Belch Greps
Believe me! Gloib mir!
Belles lettres Shaineh literatur
Belly-button Pipek, pupik
Beloved Basherter (fated); gelibteh
Bending your ear Farblujet
Benefactor Bal-tsedokeh, nadven
Benevolence Tsedokeh
(To) Berate Derniderriken
Betrothal T'no'im, shidech
Bewildered Farmisht, tsemisht, tsetumelt, farblondjet
Big bargain Groisseh metsieh

89

Big boss! Balebos

Big breadwinner! (Sarcastically said of a person who isn't) Groisser fardiner! Parnosseh gebber!

Big deal! Ain klainikeit! (derisive expression; a small matter); gantseh megillah, groisseh gedillah; tararam; (sarcastically, about someone else) A gilch hot dich getrofen!

Big eater Fresser

Big healthy damsel Gezinteh moid!

Big hand Lapeh

Big mouth (sarcastic) Pisk, gembeh

Big noise Tararam

Big prick! Grossier potz! (taboo)

Big producer! (who doesn't produce) Shvitser!

Big shot (who thinks he's a big shot) Yatebedam; groisser gornisht; groisser potz (derogatory and taboo)

Big shot (big wheel) K'nacker; gantser k'nacker; groisser shisser; macher

Big talker, little doer! Pisk-malocheh!

Big thing! A glick ahf dir! (sarcastically used for little good fortunes that occur)

Bit Shtik, shtikel

Bit of acting A shtik

Bitter person Farbissener

Blabbermouth (female) Yenteh

(A) Black year! A shvartz yor!

Blasphemous person Grober yung, grobyon, grubyon

Bless ye! Boruchu! (Hebrew)

Blessed Zelig

Blessed be God! Boruch hashem (Hebrew)

Blessed with children Gebentsht mit kinder

Blessing over bread Hamoitzeh. The full blessing is: Borunch ato adonoi elo-hainu melech oilom hamotzi le-chem min ho'orets.

Blessing over wine Kiddish. The full blessing is: Boruch ato adonoi elo-hainu melech oilom borai pri hagofen.

Blinding the eyes! Shvindilt in di oygen!

Blockhead! (Ass!) Chamoyer, du ainer!

Blues singer Krechtser

Blundering Farblondjet

(A) Blusterer Yatebedam

Boarding house with cooking privileges Kochalain

Boil Makeh

Boisterer Tumler; shaigets, shkotz

Bologna Vursht

Bon mot Gleichvertel

Bon voyage For gezunterhait! Gai gezunterhait!

(The) Book of services for the first two nights of Passover Hagadah

Boor Yold, amo'orets, amorets, poyer

Boorish young man Gruber yung

Boorish or coarse person Bulvan

Bore Nudnik

Born loser Shlimazel; umglicklecher

Borsht circuit The Catskill mountains where there are so many Jewish hotels (see Yiddish-English section)

Boss Balhabos (pl., balalbatim); balebos

(To) Bother Tshepen, bareh

Bothersome hanger-on Ontshepenish, tsutshepenish

Boy (affectionate) Boitshik, boitshikel (Americanism); yingel

Boy (becoming a man) Bar-mitzvah

Braggart Barimer, shvitser, ois'shteler, umshteller

Brand-new Shpogel nei.

Brave Mutik heldish; brahv; shtark

Brazenness Chutzpeh

Break a leg! Brech a fus!

Break wind Fortz, fortzen (taboo)

Breast Tsitskeh (taboo), brist, brust

(To) Bribe (slang) Shmeer, unterkoifen, geben shoy-chad

Bridal canopy Chupeh

Bride Kalleh

Bride and groom Chossen-kalleh

Bridegroom Chossen

Bright saying Chochmeh

Broker Mekler (fem., meklerkeh)

Brothel Bordel, shandhoiz, heizel

Brother-in-law Shvoger

Brown-noser Tocheslecker (taboo)

91

(A) Brunhilde Gezunteh moid
Buckwheat Kasheh
Buffoon Shmegegi, yold, shmendrik, yukel
Bum Trombenik
Bum (he) Bohmer (Americanism)
(she) Bohmerkeh (Americanism)
Bungler Klotz, shlemiel, shlimazel, tsedaiter kop
Burst! Plats!
Burglar Ganef, goniff
Burp Grepts
Burst with frustration Platsen
(To) Bury Bagroben
Business Geshefts
(The) Business (as, giving you . . .) Shmeeren, on-zaltzen
Bust! Plats!
Bust your guts out! Plats!
(To) Bust Platsen
(A) Busy-body Kochleffel
Butter-fingered Shlemiel
(To) Butter up Untershmeichlen, shmeichel
Buttocks Toches, hinten, inten; tush (only applied to infant)
Button K'neppel, k'nop
Buxom girl Moid; gezunteh moid; zaftikeh moid
By all means! Aderabeh-ve'aderabeh

Cancer-shmancer, as long as you're healthy Cancer-shmancer, abi gezunt

Candlestick (seven-branched) Menorah, menoireh

Cantor Chazen

Cantor's singing Tsiklen zich

Capable housewife and homemaker (complimentary term) Balebosteh, beryeh

Careless dresser Shlump, opgelozen(er)

Carrot compote Tsimmes

(To) Carouse Hulyen

(To) Carry Shlepen

(To) Carry or pull an extra object or person Shlep, shlepen

Cash Mezuma, mezumen

Cash only! Don't ask for credit! Ribi-fish, gelt ah-fen tish!

Cash on the barrel-head! Ribi-fish, gelt ah-fen tish!

Casper Milquetoast Kunyehlemel, shnook, lemeshkeh

Casting off sins on the New Year Tashlich

Caustic greeting (used in reference to women) Skotsel kumt!

Ceremony of the casting off of sins on the New Year Tashlich

Certainly! Tahkeh!

Charity Tsdokeh

Chaste (applied to a female) Frum, opgehit, tsnueh

Chat Shmux'es

(To) Chat Shmuessen

(To) Chatter Plaplen

Chattering Reden on a moss; Yatatata

Cheap (price) Billik; (person) Parshiveh, parech, mieser nefesh, karger

Cheap as soup Billik vi borsht (a real bargain!)

Cheap skate (female) Kushinyerkeh, mark-yiddeneh

Cheap skate (male) Karger, mieser oisvorf

(To) Cheat Yentzen, opnaren

(A) Cheater Yentzer, shvindler, oisvorf

Cheated Opgenart, opgeyentzt

Cheek (impudence) Chutzpeh

Cheese or jellied pancakes rolled in dough and fried in fat Blintses

Chicken gizzards Pupiklech

Child Shtik naches (Lit., Piece of joy); kind

Child (youngest in family) Mizinikil

Childbirth amulet (or charm) Kimpet-tzettel

Children Kinder

Children (affectionate term) Kinderlech

Chiseler Shnorrer

Choke yourself! Ver dershtikt!

Cholera Chalerya, choleryeh

Chopped herring Gehakteh hering

Chopped liver Gehakteh leber

Chopped meat Hak flaish

Chronic ailment Farshlepteh krenk

Chronic complainer Pitshetsh, klogmuter (masc. and fem.)

Chump Yold

Circumcision, (the ceremony of circumcision) Bris, bris mieleh

Circumcisor (man who performs ritual of circumcision) Mohel

Clever fellow Molodyets

94

Clumsy bungler Shlemiel, kunyeh-lemel, lemeshkeh, shlimazel

Clumsy, sluggish person (robot-type) Golem, goilem

Clumsy person Klotz, kunyehlemel, shlemiel, shmendrek, shlimazel, lemeshkeh

Clutched at my heartstrings Klemt mir beim hartz

Cluttered Ongepatschket, ongervarfen

Coachman Balagoleh

Coarse Grob, prost

(A) Coarse person Grober yung, bulvan, grober, prostak, grubyan

Coarse, loud-mouthed woman Yachneh, yenteh

Coat like butter (bribe) Shmeer

Coat (long) worn by ultra religious Jews Kaftan

Coffee cake (like Danish pastry) Shnecken

Cold spinach soup Tshav

Colleague Chaver (pl., chavairim)

Come in! Arein! Kumt arein!

Come now! Gait, gait!

(To) Come to mind Tsu kumen oifen zinen

Come to the point! Mach es kalechdik un shpitzik! Nit gandjet!

Come-upper Oyfgekumener; olreitnik (Americanism)

Commandment Mitzveh, di (-s)

Commandment to study the law Talmud torah

Commemoration service of the dead Yiskor

Common Prost

Common man Proster mentsh

Common people Prosteh leit, proster oilem, hamoyn

Common sense; good sense Saichel; mit a kop oif the plaitses

Communal busybody Shlatten-shammes

Company (of people) Chevreh

Compassion Rachmones

Competent housewife Balebosteh, beryeh

Complain K'vetsh, klogen

Complainer K'vetsher, klogmuter (male and fem.)

Complaint (of a novel sort) A chissoren, di kaleh is tsu shain

Complete details   Gantseh megilleh (slang)

Compulsive eater   Fresser

Comrade   Chaver (pl., chavairim)

(To) Con   Shmeikel

Conceited   Ongeblozzen, grois-halter, ba'al gaiveh

Confused   Tsemisht, tsetumelt, tsedrumshket

Confusing (work)   Ongepatshket

Confusion (noise)   Tumel, tsemishnich

Confusion (mix-up) (slang)   Kasheh, mishmash

Conglomeration   Kakapitshi

Congratulations!   Mazel-tov!

Conniver   Draikop

Connoisseur   Maivin

Continuous eater of delicacies   Nasher

Conversation   Shmu'es

Cooked groats and broad noodles   Kasheh varnishkes

Coquette   Pitshetsheh, koketkeh

Corny   Shmaltzy

Costly   Teier

Could be!   Ken zein! Efsher!

Countryman   Lantsman, landsman (a fellow townsman from the old country)

Country peddler   Karabelnick, hoizirer

Cow   Behaimeh (sarcastically, dull-witted person)

Cracklings   Gribbenes (or grivvenes, greeven)

Craze   Meshugahss

Crazy   Meshugeh, tsedrait

Crazy antics   Meshugahss

Crazy as a loon!   Meshugeh ahf toi't!

Crazy bastard!   Meshugener mamzer!

Crazy man   Meshugener

Crazy woman   Meshugeneh

(A) Crazy world   A meshugeneh velt!

Crepe suzettes   Blintses

Criminal, murderer, racketeer (depending on your point of view)   Gazlen untervelt mentsh

Cripple   Kalyekeh

Critic who criticizes things that don't exist or that are uncriticizable   Er kricht oyf di gleicheh vent!

Crook   Ganef

Crooked actions Genaivisheh shtiklech

Cross-eyed Kasokeh, kosokeh

Crude Grob

Crude person Grober yung, grobyan, grubyan

Cry for help Oi g'vald! or just plain "G'vald!!!!"

Cry of anguish Oi, g'vald!

Cry of distress for help (Lit., force, violence) G'vald!!

Cry of suffering, or frustration Oi, g'vald!

Curse Choleryah, makeh, shlok; a broch! A finster yor! An umglik! A finsternish!

Cursed, accursed Geshtroft

Curses A broch! A klog!

Customary gifts exchanged on Purim (usually goodies) Shalach mohnes

Cut it short! Un langeh hakdomes! Shpitz bekitzur!

Cut-rate store Shlak joint (Americanism)

Cute (like a girl) Tsatskeh

D

Daddy Tateh, tatteh, tatteleh, tatinkeh, tatteniu
Daily Tog-teglech
Daily prayer book Sidder
Dairy dietary law Milchiks (milk product foods must
  not be eaten at same meal with meat (flaishik) foods);
  (adj.) Milchikeh or milichdik
Dairy foods Milchiks (of milk base content); milechiks
Damn it! A broch!
Danger Sakoneh
Dangerous Geferlech, sakoneh
Darling Neshomeleh, teiers
Darling son Zuninkeh
Daughter Bas (Hebrew); tochter (Yiddish)
Daughter-in-law Shnur
David's shield Mogen David
Day-to-day Tog-teglech
Dead hungry Toit hungerik
Dear Teier
Dear me! Oi vai!
Dear son Zunin-keh
Debauchee Hultei, veibernik
Decayed Forfoilt, tsefoilt
Deception Shvindel, opnarerei

98

Decorated (beautified) Pysgeputst, fartrasket, oisgesh-trozelt

Decorative (something) Putskeh

Decrepit person or thing Tranteh altvarg, noiteh lomus

Deep sorrow or hurt Fardross

(To) Defecate Kucken (taboo)

Defecate on him! Kuck im on (taboo)

Defecator Kucker (taboo)

Delicacy Meichel

Delicious Tsegait zich in moyl

Delicious tasting Geshmak, mecheieh, mecheiehdik

Delight Naches, hanoeh, fraid, fargenigen

(To be) Delighted K'velen

(To be) Destined Bashert zein

Devout Frum (frimer)

Dietary laws Kashress

Diminutive suffixes El, eleh

Diminutive, affectionate term for children Kinderlech

(To) Dine Essen mitek

Dingus Tsatskeh

Diplomacy Saichel, diplomatyeh

Dipped Toonked, tunked, eingetunken

Dirt Shmuts

Dirty Shmutsik

Disappointment Ahntoisht, zich filen opgenart

Disappointment Ahntoishung, fardross

Disbelief, distaste, contempt Phooey! Fuie! Fu zol es veren!

Disdain (exclamation) Pooh!

(In) Disgrace and humiliation. Tsu shand un tsu shpot

Disgust (exclamation) Oi! (Please say this in a disgusting way—with a grunt-like sound coming deep from the throat!)

Disgusting fellow Paskudnik, paskudnyak, ekeldiker parshoyn

Dismay Oi vai!

Disordered Ongepatshket, ongevarfen

Distressed Fardeiget

Divorce Get

Dizzy Shvindeldik

(Feeling) Dizzy   Shvindilt in di oygen

(To) Do all the talking   A braiteh daieh hoben

Do it fast!   Maches shnel!

Do it for my sake.   Tu mir tsulib.

Do me a favor.   Tu mir a toiveh. Tu mir tsulib.

Do me a favor and drop dead!   Folg mich a gang un gai in dr'erd!

(To) Do things in time-wasting manner   Patshken

Do you want?   Vilstu?

Does it matter to you?   S'art eich?

Doesn't worry.   Nishtgedeiget

Doll   Tsatskeh, krassavitseh, yefayfiyeh

Dolt   Shnook, shlepper, temp

Done in!   Opgeflickt

Donkey, you!   Chamoyer du ainer!

Don't annoy me!   Bareh mich nit!

Don't ask for credit!   Ribi-fish, gelt ahfen tish!

Don't be a damn fool!   Zei nit kain vyzosoh!

Don't be a fool!   Zei nit a nar! Zei nit kain goylem!

Don't be an idiot!   Zei nit kain vyzosoh!

Don't be silly!   Gai shoyn, gai! Zei nit kain nar!

Don't bleed me!   Tsap mir nit dos blut!

Don't bother me!   Drai mir nit kain kop! Hak mir nit kain tsheinik! Tshpeh zich nit tsu mir! Tshepeh zich op fun mir!

Don't bother me!   Gai kucken ahfen yam! (taboo) (Lit., go defecate on the ocean!)

Don't complain.   Zindik nit. Baklog zich nit.

Don't do me any favors.   Tu mir nit kain toives.

Don't double talk.   Nisht gefonfet. Fonfeh nit.

Don't fool around.   Nisht gefonfet; bareh nit! (taboo)

Don't fornicate around.   Bareh nit! (taboo)

Don't get excited!   Shat, shat. Se brent nit!

Don't give me a canary; (don't give me an evil eye).   Gib mir nit kain einhoreh

Don't hedge.   Nisht gefonfet.

Don't make a big deal out of it!   Mach nit kain tsimmes fun dem!

Don't mix things up!   Farmisht nit di yoytzres!

Don't screw me around.   Bareh mich nit.

Don't sin! Zindik nit!

Don't tempt fate. Zindink nit

Don't threaten me! Strasheh mich nit!

Don't twist my head! Drai mir nit kain kop!

Don't worry! Deigeh nisht! Hob nit kain deiges! Nishtgedeiget! Zorg zich nit!

Dope Shmendrik, yold, chamoyer, eizel, nar

Dopey, clumsy person Shlemiel

Doo-dad Tshatshki, tsatskeh

(To) Double-talk. Funfen, fonfen

Dowdy, gossipy woman Shlepperkeh, rechielesnitseh

Down the hatch! Le'chayim, l'chei-im

Dowry Nadan

Drab Nebbish, nebach

(To) Drag, carry or haul (particularly unnecessary things or parcels) Shlepen

Dreary Kalamutneh

Dressed up (to the hilt!) Oysgeputst

Dried Gedarteh, dareh

Driver Balagoleh

Drop dead! Geharget zolstu veren! Ver derharget! Ver geharget! Zolst ligen in drerd! Lig in drerd! Ich hob dich! (mildest)

Drummer in a band Barabantshik

Drunk Shikker

Drunkard Shikker

Drunken, inebriated Shikker, farshnoshket

Ducky (swell, pleasant) Katshkedik

Dull person, clumsy and sluggish Goilem

Dull-witted Behaimeh, poyer

Dullard Temper kop, poyer

Dumb like a piece of wood! Shtik holtz?

Dumbell! Dumkop!

Dumplings (round and cooked) K'naidlech (flat, filled and baked) K'nishes

Dunce Dumkop

Dung Drek (taboo)

Dungy Farkakteh, fekuckteh

Dunked Tunked, toonked, eingetunken

101

(To) Earn a blessing (by doing a good deed) Fardinen a mitzveh

East Mizrach

Eastern Mizrach

Eastern wall in synagogue Mizrach vant

Eat in good health! Ess gezunterhait!

(To) Eat like a pig! Fressen vi a chazzer!

Eccentric (man) Meshuggener, tsedreiter
  (woman) Meshuggeneh, tsedreiteh

Egghead (talmudic) Batlen

Eggs Baitsim (taboo), aier

Either too much or not enough. Oder a klop, oder a fortz (taboo)

Elite Feinshmeker, meyuches, choshever mentsh

Emaciated Oysgedart, oysgetsert

Embittered Farbissener

End of the world! Ek velt!

Endearing suffix -Niu; el, eleh

Endearing term (for anybody you like, young or old) Bubeleh, bubbee, tsatskeleh

Enema Kaneh, cristiyer, cristiyah

(To) Engage (hire) Dingen

Engaged couple Chossen-kalleh

Enjoy Shepen naches

Enough is enough!   Genug is genug!

Erudite person   Lamden

Esteem   Koved, derech erets

Every person has his own idiosyncrasies.   Yeder mentsh hot zeineh aigener meshugahssen.

Evil eye   Einhoreh

Excited   Tsekocht

Excitable person   Kasnik, keisnik, hitskop, farbrenter

Exclamation of disgust, pain, astonishment or rapture   Oi!!

Exclamation of surprise, dismay or disapproval   Och! Oh!

Exclamation of disdain   Pooh!

Excrement (human)   Drek (taboo)

Excuse me.   Zeit (mir) moychel. Antshuldik mir.

Exhausted   Oysgehorevet, farmutshet.

Expensive   Teier

Expert   Maivin, mumcheh

Expression of dismay   Oy, vai! (vai means pain)

Expressman   Balagoleh

Extreme pleasure   Grois fargenigen

Fag Faigeleh (taboo)
(To) Faint Chaleshen
Fainted Gechahlesht
Faintness Chaloshes
Fairness Yoysher
Fairy tale Bobbeh meisseh
Fait accompli! A nechtiker tog! Farfallen!
Faith-healer Bal Shem
Faker Trombenik, zhulyik
Fall guy Shlumpf; seir l'azozel (Hebrew for scapegoat)
False or forced laugh Lachen mit yash-tsherkis
Family Mishpocheh
Family affairs Mishpocheh-zachen
Fan Focher, fochah
Fanny (buttocks) Inten, hinten, toches (taboo)
Farewell! Zei(t) gezunt!
Farmer Yishuvnik, poyer
Fart (taboo) Fortz (taboo)
(To) Fast-talk Shmeikel
Fat Shmaltz (grease or oil compounds)
Fat Fet (robust, plump)

104

Fated Bashert

(The) Fated one; the destined one Basherter

Father Tateh, tatteh, tatteleh, tatinka, tatteniu, foter

Father-in-law Shver

Fatigued Farmutshet

Feces (Dung) Drek (taboo)

Feeble-minded Tam chosser daieh; tamavateh

Feeding rabbinnical students Essen teg

Feeling dizzy Shvindilt in di oygen

Fellow (young) who assumes airs Gantser mentsh

Female Nekaiveh (also means tart or whore)

Female Angel of Death Malech-hamovesteh

Female blabbermouth Yenteh

Female broker Meklerkeh

Female demon Klipeh

Female infant (affectionate term) Pisherkeh (taboo; Lit., Little urinator)

Female tricks Veiberisheh shtik

Festive Yontenfdik

Fever Kadoches, feeber, hitz

Fidgety Zitsen ahf shpilkes

Fiftieth Wedding Anniversary Goldeneh chasseneh

Fighter (usually for a cause) Kemfer

Filthy rich Ongeshtopt mit gelt

Finally Sok-kol-sof

(A) Find (bargain) Metsieh

Fine (upstanding) Balebatish

Finicky Aidel gepatshket; prietskeh (refers only to a girl)

Finished! A nechtiker tog!

First two words of mourner's prayer for the dead Yisgadal, vyiskadash

Five dollar bill Finef, finferl

Flattery Shmaltz (slang); drek (taboo)

(To) Flatulate Fortzen (taboo)

Flatulence Fortz (taboo)

Flavor Ta'am

(To) Fleece Yentz, opnaren

Floorshow Kabaret forshtelung

Folly Shmontses

105

Food forbidden under Jewish dietary laws Traif, traifeh
Food that meets rules of Jewish dietary laws Kosher
Fool Nar; slang—shlemiel, shmendrik, shmegegi, be-haimeh, ferd, yold
Fool (self-made) Shmok (taboo)
Fooled Opgenart
Foolish Narish
(A) foolish, dumb person Shlump, shlub, zhlub
Foolish (fruitless) question Klotz kasheh
Foolishness Narishkeit
Fooey! Feh!
For a change! In a noveneh!
For better, for worse Tsum glik, tsum shlimazel
For nothing Umzist
For the sake of Vegen
Forbidden food Traif
Forbidden literature Traifeneh bicher, traifeneh literatur
Forget him! Ich hob im in bod!
Forget it! A nechtiker tog! (idiom) Fargess es! (Lit.)
Forgetful Katzisher kop, katz-in-kop
Forgive me Zeit (mir) moychel
(To) Fornicate Baren, trenen, yentzen (all taboo)
Fornicator (taboo) Yentzer
Fracture Broch
Fractured English Gebrochener english; gehakteh english
Fraud Shvindel
(A) free-loader Shlepper, shnorrer
Free-thinking Jew Apikoiress, goy
Free-thinking Jewish girl Apikoiresteh, goyeh
Fried chicken skin or fat Gribbenes, grivvenes, greeven
Friend (male) Chaver (pl., chavairim)
  (fem.) Chaverteh
Friendly face Haimish ponim
Friendly term for anybody you like Bubbee (booh-bee)
Frig you! (taboo) Tren zich! (taboo)
Fringed garment Tsitseh-kanfes, talis koten
Fringed sleeveless shirt Leibtsudekel
Fringes attached to the four corners of the tallis (prayer shawl) Tsitsis, tzitz

106

From your mouth to God's ear!   Fun dein moyl in Gots
   oyern!

Front row in the synagogue   Mizrach-vant

Frozen   Farfroyren

Fruit and nut coffee rolls   Shnecken

Fruitless, endless matter   Farshlepteh krenk

Full of care, anxiety   Fardeiget

Funeral   Levei-yah

(To) Futz around   Patshken

(A) Fuss over nothing   Machen a tsimmes

Gabby, talkative, shrewish woman Yenteh, klipeh
Gadabout Kochleffel
Gall (impudence) Chutzpeh
Garden of eden, paradise Ganaiden
Gargle solution Haldz-shvenkechts
Gather pleasure Shepen naches
Gentile Goy
Gentile boy Shaigetz (pl., shkotzim)
Gentile woman Goyeh
Gentle Gemitlich
Get a move on! Gib zich a shockel! Gib zich a traisel!
  Eilt zich!
Get away from me! Tshepeh zich op fun mir!
Get killed! Ver derharget! Ver geharget!
Get lost! Go away! Ver farblondjet! Trog zich op!
Get lost! Gai kucken ahf dem yam (taboo; **Lit.,**
  defecate in the ocean)
(To) Get rid of Obtshepen zich
Getting senile Aiver butel, veren oiver botel
Gimmick Machareikeh
Girl of marriageable age Kalleh moid
Gizzard Pipek, pupik
Glass of tea Glezel tai
Gloomy Kalamutneh, kalemutneh

(To) Glow with pride and happiness   K'velen

(A) Gnawing, grinding person   Grizhidiker

Go away!   Gai avek!

Go away, get lost!   Ver farblondjet!

Go bang your head against the wall!   Gai klop zich kop in vant!

Go-between (male)   Mekler
   (fem.)   Meklerkeh

Go bother the bedbugs!   Gai bareh di vantsen!

Go break a leg!   Gai tsebrech a fus!

Go break your own head!   Shlog zich kop in vant!

Go drive yourself crazy!   Gai fardrai zich dein (aigenem) kop!

Go drive yourself crazy, then you'll know how I feel.   Fardrai zich dein kop, vest du mainen s'iz meiner!

Go fight City Hall!   Shlog zich mit Got arum! Gai shlog zich mit Got arum!

Go fight heaven!   Gai shlog zich mit Got!

Go flap your ears!   Ich hob dich!

Go frig yourself!   Gai tren zich (taboo)

Go jump in a lake!   Nem zich a vaneh!

Go mix yourself up, not me!   Gai fardrai zich dein aigenem kop!

Go peddle your fish elsewhere!   Gai feifen ahfen yam!

(To) Go somewhere unwillingly or unwantedly   Shlepen zich

Go split your guts!   Gai plats!

Go take a bath!   Nem zich a vaneh!

Go take a shit for yourself (taboo)   Kuck zich oys! (taboo)

Go to hell!   Gai in drerd arein! Ich hob dich in drerd! Gai kabenyah mattereh!

Go to the devil!   A ruach in dein taten's taten arein!

Goad   Utz

God   Oybershter; der Oybershtern himmel; Got

God damn it!   A broch!

God forbid! (It shouldn't happen!)   Cholileh! Got zol ophiten! Nishtu gedacht! Chas v'cholieh Chas v'sholem! Umbeshrien! Umberufen!

God in Heaven, Master of the Universe. Riboynoy-Shel Olyom! (Hebrew)

God in Heaven! Got in himmel! (said in anguish, despair, fear or frustration); also, Oybershter in himmel!

God knows Got vaist

God, our Father Tateniu-Foter

God should hear you and favor you! Fun eier moyl in Gots oyeren!

God watches out for fools! Got hit op di naronim

God will it! Alivei! Halevai!

God will punish! Got vet shtrofen!

God willing! Mirtsishem (contraction of Im yirtseh Hashem)

Going into labor to give birth Gaien tsu kind

Golden country Goldeneh medineh (usually refers to the United States)

Gonorrhea Tripper

Good-bye Zei(t) gezunt. (A) Guten tog. Gai gezunterhait! A guten!

Good-day (A) Guten tog

Good deed Mitsveh

(A) Good-for-nothing Groisser gornisht

Good for nothing! Toig ahf kapores!

Good health! Gezunt-heit!

Good health to you! A gezunt ahf dein kop!

Good holiday! Gut yontev!

Good Jew Shainer Yid

Good luck! Zol zein mit glick! Mazel tov!

Good luck to you! A glick ahf dir!

Good Sabbath! Gut Shabbes

Good taste Ta'am

Good things (food, dollars, news, etc.) Guts (gits)

Gooey food Shmaltz, shmaltzik

(A) Goof Shmoe (Americanism)

Goofy parents, goofy children Meshgueneh gens, memeshugeneh gribenes

(A) Gossip Yachneh, yenteh; rechilesnutzeh; plyotkenitzeh

(To) Gossip Shushken zich, bareden yenem

(A) Gourmand   Fresser

Gourmandizing   Fressing (Americanism)

Gourmet's delight   Meichel

Grace at meals   Bentshen; birchas hamozoin (Hebrew)

Grandchild   Ainikel; shtik naches (fig.)

Grandfather   Zaideh

Grandmother   Bobbeh

Grandmother's story (figuratively, a fairy tale, an unbelievable story)   Bobbeh meiseh, baba meiseh, bub-
   beh meiseh

Gratification (from children)   Naches

Grease (fat)   Shmaltz

Great!   Ei, gut!

(A) Great pleasure (usually food)   Mecheieh!

(A) Great pleasure (to meet you)   A fargenigen (tzu
   eich bagaigenen)

Great satisfaction   Mecheieh

Groan   Ech! (of disgust); oy, vai! (of distress)

Groans   Krechts

Groats   Kasheh

Growl   Burtshen

(To) Guard   Varfen an oyg

(A) Guilty person is always sensitive   Ahfen goniff brent
   dos hittel

Guy who doesn't smell too good   Shtunk, shtinker

(A) Hag (also worthless) Shkapeh
Hanger-on Shlepper, nuchshlepper, tsutsheppenish
Happiness Naches, frailechkeit
Happy Frailech
Happy-go-lucky people A lebedikeh velt
Happy Sabbath! Gut shabbos!
Hard Shver
Hard circular roll with hole in the center like a doughnut Bagel, baigel
Hard doughnut with glazed surface Bagel, baigel
Hard-luck guy Shlimazel
Hard-luck sucker Shlimazel
Hard-working, efficient housewife Beryeh
(To) Haul Shlepen
(To) Have a yen for Farglist, farglust, glusten tsu, hoben chaishek tsu
(To) Have no end of trouble Hoben tsu zingen un tsu zogen
Have respect! Hob derech erets!
Have you finished the dirty work? Shoyn opgetrent? (taboo) (Lit., Have you finished fornicating?)
Having a ball! Laibt a tog! Leben a guten tog!
He aspires to higher places (beyond his reach) Er kricht in di hoyecheh fenster

112

He doesn't give a damn!   Es ligt im nit in zinnen. Er hot es in drerd.

He doesn't know what he's looking at!   Er kukt vi a hun in a B'nai Odom!

He eats like a horse.   Er frest vi a ferd.

He eats as if just recovered from a sickness.   Er est vi noch a krenk.

He has a cold.   Er hot a farshtopteh nonyeh. Er iz farkilt.

He has odd ways.   Er hot modneh drochim Er pravhet meshugeneh shtik.

He has no say (authority)   Er hot nit kain daieh!

He has nothing!   Er hot kadoches!

He has nothing at all.   Er hot a makeh (boil)!

He hasn't got a worry!   Er hot nit kain zorg!

He makes a lot of trouble for me.   Er macht mir a shvartzeh chasseneh! Er tut mir on tsores.

He makes a mess.   Er farkocht a kasheh.

He-man   Mentsh, parshoin

He repeats himself; (he re-hashes things over and over again)   Er molt gemolen mel.

He ruins it.   Er macht a tel fun dem.

He should burn up!   A feier zol im trefen! Brenen zol er!

He should drop dead!   Paigeren zol er!

He should go to hell!   Er zol einemen a miesseh meshuneh! A gehenem oif ihm!

He should grow like an onion, with his head in the ground.   Er zol vaksen vi a tsibeleh, mit dem kop in drerd.

He should have lots of trouble!   A meisseh meshuneh! Alleh tzores oif zein kop!

He talks himself into a sickness!   Er redt zich ein a krenk!

He talks nonsense!   Er redt in der velt arein. Er bolbet narishkeiten.

He turns the world upside down!   Er kert iber di velt!

Head of a family   Balhabos, balebos, broitgeber, farzorger

Headache   Kop vaitik

Healthy as a horse   Gezunt vi a ferd

Hear ye!   Shema (Hebrew)

113

Heart ache Harts vaitik
Heartbroken Tsebrochen harts
Hearty laugh Hartsik, shaineh gelechter
Heavy Shver
Hebrew school for children Talmud Torah
(The) Hell with him! Kuck im on! (taboo)
Hello Sholem aleichem, shalom!
Help! G'vald!
Here, take it (in giving) Na!
Here's to you! (toast) L'chei-im!
He's a low down, good-for-nothing! Er iz a nider-
 rechtiker kerl!
He's a nothing! Shmegeggi!
He's (it's) gone! Forget it! A nechtiker tog!
He's hardly (barely) alive Kam vos er lebt
He's restless! Er zitst oyf shpilkes!
He's slow as molasses! Er kricht vi a vantz!
He's so happy! Braiter vi lainger! Er iz azoy frailech!
He's thick Er hot a farshtopten kop
He's thick-headed Er hot a farshtopteh kop
He's worthless Er toyg ahf kapores
Hifalutin Feinshmeker
Hick Yold
Highly connected person Yachsen
Highly excitable person Farshmei-iter, shvebeleh (Lit., a
 match)
(To) Hire Dingen
Hodgepodge Mishmash, kasheh
Hoi polloi Mittelmeissiker
Hold on! (wait) Vart! S'teitsh!
Hole Loch
Hole in the head Loch in kop
Holiday Yontev, yontiff, yomtov
Holiday-ish Yontefdik
Homeless wandering Valgeren zich
Homosexual Faigeleh (taboo)
Honor Koved
Honorable Balebatish
Horrible ending Finsteren sof
Horrible year Finster yor

114

Horse Ferd

Host Balabos (pl., balaibatim)

Hot bath Haiseh vanneh

Hot-head Kasnik, keisenik, hitsik

Hostess who serves you meagerly, gives you A lek un a shmek

Householder Balabos (pl., balaibatim); balebos

Housewife (efficient and competent) Beryeh, balebosteh

How are things? Vi gaits? Vos hert zich?

How are things (with you)? Vi gait es (eich)?

How are you? (sing.) Vos machstu? *(pl.)* Vos macht ir?

How come? Viazoy? S'teitsh!

How do you do? Sholem alaichem! Vos macht ir?

How else? Vi den?

How goes it? Vi gaits? Vos hert zich?

How goes it with you? Vi gait es eich?

How is that? S'teitsh?

How is that possible! S'teitsh?

How much? Vifil?

How should I know? Freg mir becherim!

How's business? Vi gait dos gesheft?

How's tricks? Vi gaits? Vos hert zich?

(To) Humble somebody Derniderriken

Hurry up! Eilt zich! Mach shnel! Nu, shoyn? Yogt zich unter!

Hush! Quiet! Shat, shat!

Hymen K'nippel (taboo); b'sulim

I am disappointed. Ich bin ahntoisht. Ich fil zich opgenart.

I'm dying for it! Mein cheiyes gait oys noch dem!

I am fainting! Es vert mir finster in di oygen. Ich gai chaleshen!

I am in a hurry. Ich eil zich.

I'm not in a hurry. Ich yog zich nit.

I'm sorry. Es tut mir bahng.

I defecate on him (usually said about someone you're angry with, disgusted with, or rejected) Ich kuck ahf im. (taboo)

I despise you! Ich hob dich in bod! Ich feif oif dir!

I did wrong! So call me a "nut." Ruf mich k'nak-nissel

I don't envy you Ich bin dich nit mekaneh

I don't give a care! A deigeh hob ich! S'art mich vi di vant!

I don't give a hang! A deigeh hob ich!

I don't know. Ich vais nit.

I dream of Es cholemt zich mir

I hate him. Ich hob im feint.

I have a choice? A braireh hob ich?

I have a heartburn. Iz brent mir ahfen hartz.

116

I have him in my buttocks! (usually said about someone you don't care for, or angry with)   Ich hob im in to-ches! (taboo)

I have no use for it.   Ich darf es ahf kapores.

I haven't the faintest idea!   Zol ich azoy vissen fun tsores! Ich zol azoy vissen fun baiz!

I have you in hell! Go to hell!   Ich hob dich in drerd!

I know.   Ich vais.

I like it. It pleases me.   Es gefelt mir.

I need it like a hole in my head   Ich darf es vi a loch in kop

I need it like a wart on my nose.   Ich darf es vi a lung un leber oif der noz.

I predicted it (my heart told me)   Dos hartz hot mir gezogt

I should have such a year!   Az a yor ahf mir!

I should have such good luck!   Az glick ahf mir!

I should know from trouble (as little as I know about what you are asking me).   Ich zol azoy vissen fun tsores.

I should worry.   A deigeh hob ich.

I wish it could be said about me.   Ahf mir gezogt.

(An) Idea occurred to me.   Es iz mir eingefalen a plan.

Idiot   Shmegegi, vyzoso (both slang); idiyot

(To) Idle   Shlump (slang)

Idler   Laidik gaier; batlen (if he's a perpetual scholar); pustunpasnik

Ignoramus   Am-ho'orets, amorets

Ignorant boor   Prostak, poyer

Ignorant Jew   Goy, shtik goy, grobber kop

Ignorant people   Prosteh mentshen

I'll give you nothing!   Ich vel dir geben kadoches!

I'm dying for it!   Mein cheies gait oys!

I'm not in a hurry   Ich yog zich nit. Ich eil zich nit.

I'm sorry   Es tut mir bahng. Es tut mir laid.

Impossible!   A nechtiker tog! Ummeglich!

Impudent fellow   Chutzpenik, ahzes ponim

Impure food (contrary to dietary laws)   Traif, nit kosher

In, into   Arein

In disgrace and humiliation   Tsu shand un tsu shpot

117

In good health Gezunterhait

In-law Mechuten

In-laws Mechutonim

In spite of everything you do, it still comes out wrong Aft tsi'lehaches, ahf tseloches

In the middle of In miten drinen

In a pig's eye! A nechtiker tog!

In the rear Fun hinten; in hinten

In trouble Ahf tsores

Incompetent person (who has perpetual bad luck) Shlimazel, loy yitslach

Inept person Shlemiel

Inexpensive Billik

Inferior Shlub, tandaitneh

Inferior merchandise or work. Drek (taboo); par- tatshnek

Innocent Got di neshomeh shuldik; nit shuldik

Insane Meshugeh ahf toyt; meshugeh tsum toyt

Insanity Meshugahas

Insignificant mistake Bubu

Insincere talk Falsheh raid. Drek (taboo)

Inspector or supervisor of Kashreth (Kashress) in restaurants or hotels who makes sure everything is kosher Mashgiach

Integrity Yoysher

Intercourse (sexual) Zetz, shtup (taboo)

(To) Irk Tshepen

Irreligious Jew Apikoires; shtik goy

Irreligious Jewish boy. Shaigetz shkotz.

Irreligious Jewish girl. Shikseh.

Is he bewildered! Er drait zich vi a fortz in rossel. (ta- boo)

Is he in a fog! Er drait zich vi a fortz in rossel. (taboo)

Is it? Tsi?

Is it my worry? A deigeh hob ich?

Is that how you talk to a father? Azoy ret men tsu a taten?

Is that so? Azoy zugstu? Takeh?

It appears to me Es veist zich mir oys

It could be! Es ken zein.

It doesn't make sense! Es iz nit geshtoigen un nit gefloigen.

It doesn't matter. S'macht nit oys.

It doesn't matter to me. Es macht mir nit oys.

It doesn't work! Es gait nit! Gaiet es nit! Se arbet nit!

It gives me a great pleasure! Es tut mir a groisseh hanoeh! Se git mir a groisseh ano-eh (often said sarcastically)

It gives me pleasure Es tut mir hanoeh. (often said sarcastically.) Es git mir a (groissen) fargenigen.

It hurts me. Es tut mir vai.

It is conceivable Es ken gemolt zein

It is imaginable Es ken gemolt zein.

It is (too) late. Es iz (tsu) shpet.

It is not becoming Es past nit.

It is revealed Veist oys

It is said Me zogt

It is very expensive (cheap). Es is Zaier teier (billik).

It isn't proper! Es past nit!

It isn't running smoothly! Es gait nit!

It looks like Veist oys

It makes no difference (it doesn't matter). Es mach nit oys.

It melts in your mouth! Tsegait zich in moyl.

It never happened! Es iz nit geshtoigen un nit gefloigen!

It pleases me. Es gefelt mir.

It should be well! Zol zein gut!

It should bang in your head (as it's annoying me)! Zol dir alain klapen in kop!

It should happen to me (to you)! Alvei! Ahf mir (dir) gezogt!

It should happen to me! Mirtsishem bei mir! Ahf mir gezogt gevoren!

It should happen to my enemies! Ahf maineh sonim gezogt!

It shouldn't come to pass! Nit do gidacht! Umberufen! Unbeshrien!

It shouldn't happen! Nishtu gedacht. Nit do gedacht!

It shouldn't happen to you! Nit far eich gedacht! Loi alaichem (Hebrew)

It sorrows me. Es tut mir bahng.

It stinks! Es gait a raiech! Se hert zich a raiech. Se shtinkt!

It will all work out. Es vet zich alts oyspressen.

It will heal in time for the wedding. Es vet zich oyshailen biz der chasseneh.

It will suffice. Es vet kleken.

It will take a long, long time (till Doomsday!). A yor mit a mitvoch.

It won't help (any)! Es vet heifen vi a toiten bahnkes!

It won't hurt in making a match. Es vet nit shatten tzum shiddech.

It's a pity Nebach; a rachmones

It's a shame for the children! Es iz a shandeh far di kinder!

It's a steal! A metzieh fun a ganef!

It's bad manners! Es past zich vi a patch tzu gut shabbes!

It's delicious! Me ken zich baleken! Me ken leken di finger fun dem!

It's gone! S'iz oys!

It's gone; forget it! A nechtiker tog!

It's good for nothing! Es toig ahf kapores!

It's great! S'iz mir gut!

It's hardly worth the trouble. Folg mich a gahng (scoffing statement)

It's not to the point! Es past zich vi a patsh tsu gut shabbes!

It's not true whatsoever. Nisht geshtoigen, nisht gefloigen.

It's O.K. with me! Bei mir poilst du!

It's on his (her) mind. Es ligt im (ir) in zinnen.

It's over. S'iz oys.

It's perfect! Kosher v'yosher!

It's tough to make a living! Shver tzu machen a leben!

It's useless! Gai klop zich kot in vant!

It's worth nothing Toig ahf kapores.

It's your own fault. Me hot alain ungekocht.

J

(A) Jerk Shlub, shlump
Jester at a wedding Badchan
Jew who works on Sabbath Mechalel shabbes, shabbes goy
Jewish head Yiddisher kop
Jewish holiday Yontiff, yomtov, yontev
Jewish law (book) Talmud
Jewish native of Galicia Galitsianer
Jewish parochial school Yeshivah togshul
Jewish prayer shawl Tallis
Joke Vitz, chochmeh
Joy (from children) Naches
Joyous occasion (birth, bar mitzvah, engagement, marriage, etc.) Simcheh
Juice Zaft
Jumble Mishmash
Just great! Ei, gut!
Just made it! Kam derlebt
Justice Yoysher

Kasha with noodles   Varnitshkes
Keep moving!   Drai zich!
Keep quiet!   Shveig!
Kiss my behind!   Kush mich in toches! (taboo); kush in
   toches arein (taboo)
Knock on wood! No evil eye! (some say "Don't give me a
   canary.")   Kain einhoreh (also, kain ain-einoreh).
Knot   K'nippel
*Know-it-all, who really doesn't know it all (sar-
   castic)*   Macht zich far a gantsen kenner; far a ya-
   tebbeh-dahm; K'nacher
Kosher condition   Kashress

Ladies' room Vashtsimmer far froien
Land of Israel Eretz Yisroel
Large as a mountain Grois vi a barg
Last child in family Mizinikil
Lazy man Foiler, foilyak
Leader of the Jewish religious community Rav, rov
Learned man Lamden. Talmid chochem. Ben Toyreh; Reb (used as title)
(To) Lease Dingen
Leave me alone! Loz mir tzu ru! Tshepeh zich op fun mir!
Lecherous old man Alter kucker (taboo)
Less than nothing Kadoches
Let it be! Zol zein!
Let me be in peace! Loz mich tzu ru!
Let's conclude this! Toches ahfen tish.
Let's end it! A sof! A sof!
Let's go! Nu, shoyn!
Let's have some quiet! Zol zein shtil!
Liar Ligner
Life Chei (numerical value of two Hebrew letters, cheth and yood, read together as Chei). Chei also means 18.
Lighter taper Shammes

Likewise Dos zelbeh
Listen! Her nor!
Listen here! Hert zich ein!
Lithuanian Litvak
Littered Ongevorfen
Little Bisel
Little bird Faigeleh
Little boy Boitshick (Americanism)
Little bride Kallehniu
Little cakes dipped in honey Taiglech
Little girl (affectionate term) Maideleh
Little infant (affectionate term) Pisherkeh
Little nothing Pitsvinik; klainer gornisht, banimenish
(A) Little of a fool Narishehvateh. Shtik nar.
Little ones Pitzelech
Little penis Petseleh (used only to describe infant boy!)
Little prig Klainer gornisht
Little squirt Pisher
Livelihood Parnosseh
(A) Lively person Rirevdiker; nit kain farshloffener; lebediker
Lively Russian dance Kazatskeh
(A) Lively world! A lebedikeh velt!
Living by one's wits Luftmentsh
(A) Living doll! Yingeh tzahtzkeh (young one); lyalkeh; tzatzkehleh (a very pretty or capricious one); tzatzkeh (take your choice!)
Living high off the hog Leben a chazershen tog
Loaded (drunk) Farshnoshket; ongetrunken
Loads of luck! Mazel tov!
Loafer Laidik-gaier, pustunpasnik
Long coat worn by religious Jews Kapoteh, kaftan
Long distance operator Tsevishen-shtotisheh telefonistkeh
Long, lean girl Langeh dronitzeh; hoieher drong
Long may you live! Lang leben zolt ir!
Long winter underwear Gatkes
Look at him! Kuk im nor on!
Look here, look here! Zeh nor, zeh nor!
Look out! Hit zich!

124

Loquacious Yatatata
Lost Tsemisht (confused); farfalen (physical loss)
Lot of nonsense Drek (shit; taboo)
Loudmouth Pisk!
(To) Lounge around Shlump; patterren tseit
Lousy Nisht gut
Low-class people Prosteh mentshen; prostaches
Luck Glick
Luckless person Shlimazel
Lump of sugar Shtik tsuker

M

Madness Meshugahss

Magic-worker Kishef macher, kuntzen macher, Bal Shem (Hebrew)

Make a living Machen a leben

Make a major issue out of a minor event Tsimmes

(To) Make a nothing out of you. Machen a tel fun dir.

(To) Make fun of Choyzik machen

Make it snappy! Mach es shnel!

Making a livelihood Hoben parnosseh, machen a leben (Americanism)

Making an outcry Machen a g'vald

Malaria Kadoches

Male infant Pisher (Taboo; Lit., a urinator); mentshal

Male person Mentsh; kaddishel (one who can say mourning prayers for his parents)

Malingering sickness A farshlepteh krenk (a sickness or matter that hangs on endlessly)

Man (derisive term) Shmok (taboo)

Man (with worth and dignity) Choshever mentsh

(A) Man built like an ox Bulvan

Man of distinguished lineage Yachsen

Man who assumes airs Bal ga'aveh; grois-halter

126

Man who behaves meanly, miserly, ungallantly, or vulgarly Rosheh

Man who builds castles in the air; never achieves anything Fantazyor; luftmentsh

Man who lives by his wits Luftmentsh

Man who threatens Yatebedam

A man with contacts Macher

Manana! Kum ich nit heint, ku mich morgen

Manly Gantser mentsh

Manure Drek (taboo)

(A) Mare (also worthless) Shkapeh

Marriage Chasseneh

Marriage broker Shadchen

Marriage ceremony Chupeh

Married man Baveibter

Master of ceremonies at weddings or banquets Badchan

Master of the Universe Riboynoy-shel-oylom

Match (marriage) Shidech, der (shiduchim, pl.)

Matchmaker Shadchan

May God help me! Zol Got mir helfen!

May God prevent! Zol Got op-hiten!

May he break a leg! Zol er tsebrechen a fus!

May he rest in peace. Olov hasholem.

May it be so! Alivei! Halevei!

May it not happen to you! Loi alaichem! (Hebrew); nebach

May it not happen to you! Loi aleichem! (Hebrew)

May no evil befall us! Kain einoreh! Kain ein horeh

May she rest in peace. Oleho hasholem.

May we meet on happy occasions. Mir zolen zich bagegenen ahf simches.

May you be inscribed for a good year. L'shono tova tikosevu.

May you live long. Lang leben zolt ir.

Maybe Efsher, ken zein

Mean Parshiveh

Mean, evil person Paskudnyak, parch, rosheh

Meat dietary law Flaishiks (Meat must not be eaten together with dairy (milichdik) foods).

Mechanic Shlosser, machinist

Mechanical man (robot) Goilem, golem
(To) Meddle (as a spectator) Kibbitzen
Meddlesome spectator Kibbitzer, muttelmessig
Meek person Shnok, lemeshkeh, kunye lemel
Memorial service Yiskor
Men's room Vashsimmer far menner
Mercy Rachmones
Mere bagatelle! Bobkes! Bubkes!
Mere messenger Shlatten-shammes
Mere nothing Shihi-pihi
Merit Meileh
Merrymaker at a wedding Badchan
(A) Mess (slang) Kasheh, mishmash, hekdish
(To) Mess around Patshkeh, patshken
Messenger Shik-yingel; shlatten-shammes
(A) Middleman (also a person who is neither smart nor
  dumb) Mittelmissiker
Mildew Farfoylt
Milked! Opgeflict! Arumgeflict!
(To) Mind something Varfen an oyg; halten an oyg; bal
  moifess
Miracle-worker Balnes
Miser Karger
Miserable weather Finster un glitshik
Miserable person Shlak
(To be) Miserly Zhaleven, kamtsoness
Misery Tsores
Misfit Kalyekeh
Misfortune Umglick
(A) Misfortune! (wail) Az och un vai!
Mistake (insignificant) Bubu
Miss Maidel, freilein, chaverteh
Mistress of a household Balhabosteh, balebosteh
Mix-up (slang) Kasheh, mishmash; kuckamaimie
Mixed up Tsemisht, farmisht
Mixed up emotionally Farmisht
(A) Mixture Mishmash
(A) Moaner Krechster (also means a blues singer)
Moans Krechtst (verb)
Money Gelt

128

Money (ready cash) Mezuma, mezumen

Money goes to money Gelt gait tzu gelt.

Money on the table! Ribi-fish, gelt ahfen tish!

Money thrown out Aroysgevorfen gelt

Money tied in a knot in corner of a handker-chief K'nippel

Money wasted Aroysgevorfen gelt

Moocher Shnorrer

Moron Szhlob

Morsel Shtikel

Mortally insane! Meshugeh ahf toyt!

Mother-in-law Shviger

Mother's pet (favorite) Tsatskeleh der mameh's

Mourner's prayer Kaddish

Mourning period Shiva, shiveh (seven days observed by family and friends of deceased)

Mouth (unflattering) Pisk (moyl: mouth)

Mouthpiece Pisk

Mouthwash Moil-shvenkechts

Move, already! Nu, shoyn! Gai shoyn!

Mr. Reb., chaver, bruder; freint (salutation)

Mr. Slowpoke Kam vos er kricht.

Mr. Upside Down! (person who does everything in reverse) Moisheh kapoyer

Mrs. Chaverteh, froy; madame (salutation)

Much ado about nothing Ahfen himmel a yarid

Muddled (slightly drunk) Far-shnoshket

Muddled work, picture or situation Ongepatshket, tsepatsket

(To) Mumble Preplen

Mush cereal Kasheh

My enemies should live so! Meineh sonim zolen azoy leben!

My heart told me Dos hartz hot mir gezogt

My money went down the drain. In drerd mein gelt! Dos gelt iz tserunen gevoren!

Naive   Tam, tamavateh
Naive person   Kunyehlemel, shmo (Americanism)
Narrowly achieved   Kam derlebt
Nasty fellow   Paskudnyak
Nausea   Chaloshes
Navel.   Pipek, pupik
Ne'er-do-well   Trombenik, nebechel, nebbish, nebach, shlak
Neighbor (from the old country)   Lantsman
Neither here nor there   Nit ahin, nit aher
Neutral food (neither milchdik nor flaishdik)   Parveh
Newlywed (male)   Yungermantshik
News   Yedies; neies
Nibble between meals   Nash, nashen
Nibbler, especially between meals   Nasher
Night is falling.   Nacht falt tsu.
Nincompoop   Shmendrik, kunyehlemel, shlok
No evil eye   Kain einoreh (also, kain ain-einoreh)
No good   Kockamaimie (slang); nit gut; nisht gut
No-gooder   Trombenik
No-good person   Nishgutnick, trombenik
Nobility   Yichus

(A) Nobody (male) Pisher (taboo); a gornisht; a nishtikeit (a pitiable person) Nebbish, nebach, nebechel; (a little person) Vantz (bedbug) a gornisht; a nishtikeit

Noise Tumel

Non-Jewish boy Shaigetz, shkotz (colloquial)

Non-Jewish girl Shikseh (colloquial)

Non-kosher Traif, traifeh

Nonsenses! A nechtiker tog! Drek (taboo)

Noodle dough Farfel

Noodle or bread suet pudding (frequently cooked with raisins) Kugel

Noodles Lokshen

Noodle pudding Kugel

Not a word of truth in it! A nechtiker tog! Also, nit emes

Not good Nisht gut; nit gut

Not in reality; supposedly Kloymersht

Not making sense Nit geshtoigen, nit gefloigen

Not necessary Nisht naitik

Not really at all! Chas v'cholileh!

Not so bad Nishkosheh

Not so fast! Chap nit!

Not today, not tomorrow! Nit heint, nit morgen!

Not yet Noch nisht

Nothing Gornit, gornisht

Nothing (of small value) Kreplech (slang); bobkes (slang); chei kuck (taboo)

(A) Nothing, a pitiful person Nebechel, nebbish

Nothing came of it! Es hot zich oysgelohzen a boydem!

Nothing of importance! Eh!

Nothing of value Shmek tabik (bit of snuff)

Nothing will help you! Es vet dir gornit helfen!

Nouveau riche. . . . Oyfgekumener g'vir; olreitnik (Americanism)

Nuisance Nudnik; tsutsheppenish

Nutty Tsedrait

O.K. Zaier gut; oisgetsaichent
Obey me! Folg mich!
Obnoxious person Nudnik, paskudnik, paskudnyak
(To) Offer unsolicited advices as a spectator Kibbitz, kibbitzen
Oh! Ei! Ei!
Oh, God! Gottenyu!
Oh, what a scandal! Oi, a shkandal! Oy, a skandal
O.K.! Let it be so! Zol zein azoy!
Old acquaintance Alter bakahnter
Old-fashioned taste Mein bobbeh's ta'am
(An) Old bum An alter trombenik
(An) Old man An alter kucker (taboo)
Old maid Alteh moid
Old-style orthodox Hebrew teacher in a "cheder" (one-room-school) Melamed (pl., melamdim)
Old witch Alteh machashaifeh
Old wreck Alteh trombenik
Omelet Feinkochen, feinkuchen
On the level Emmis, emmes, be'emes
On the square Emmis, emmes, be'emes
Once in a blue moon! In a noveneh!

132

One who stirs up things   Kochleffel

One who tends to confuse you   Draikop

Onions should grow from your navel!   Zol dir vaksen
tzibbeles fun pupik!

Only God knows   Nor Got vaist

Orderly person   Balebos; okuratner mentsh

Ornament   Tzatzkeh

Orthodox Hebrew teacher   Melamed

(The) Other's   Yenems

Other world   Yeneh velt, oilom habbo (Hebrew)

Ouch!   Oi, vai!

Outcast   Oysvurf

Overdressed   Oysgeputst, oisgeshtrobelt, oisgetzatzket

Overdressed woman   Oisgetzatzket; aribergechapt di
mohs

Over-praise (slang)   Shmaltz, chanifeh

Overseer   Mashgiach

Owner   Balabos (pl., palibatim); balebos

Pain Vai! vaitik
Pain (exclamation) Oi!
(Real) Pain (ouch!) Oi, vai!
Pale as a sheet (wall)! Blaich vi di vant! Veis vi kalech!
Palsy-walsy Aderabeh-ve'aderabeh
Pancakes (jellied or with cheese) Blintzes (and they must be rolled)
Panhandler Shnorrer
Pansy (male) Faigeleh
Papa Tateh, tatteh, tatteleh, tatinka, tatinkeh, tatteniu
Paradise Ganaiden (Garden of Eden)
Parasite Shnorrer
Parents Tateh-mameh
Parvenu Oyfgekumener g'vir; olreitnik (Americanism)
(To) Pass wind Fortzen (taboo)
Pastry Varenikes (special type). Gebeks.
Patience (that can endure sitting) Zitzflaish
(A) Patsy Shnook, shlumpf
Pauper Kabsten, kapsten
Pauper in seven edges (a very poor man) Kabtsen in ziben poless.
Peace Sholem

Peace be to you! Sholem alaichem!

Peanuts! (small things) Bobkes, bubkes (If you're curious, the word for nuts, also peanuts, is "nislech.")

Peasant Poyer

Peddler Hoizirer; pedler (Americanism)

Pedigree Yichus

Pee pot Pishteppel

Peeved Ongeblozzen

Peevish (pouting) Ongeblozzen

Penis Potz, shmok, shlang, shvontz, vyzoso (all taboo)

Penis (derisive and derogatory term for a man) Shmok, potz (taboo)

Shmohawk (Anglicized variant for "shmok")

Petseleh (affectionately applied to infant boy)

Perfect Kosher (slang)

Perish the thought! Cholileh!

Person from Lithuania Litvak

Person of loose morals Hultei

Person who butts into everything Kochleffel

Person who carries on work or sport in a slipshod, un-business-like, half-assed manner Patsher

Person who does not abide by Jewish law Traifener bain! Traifenik! Traifnyok! Shaigetz!

Person who will do anything to gain favor Toches-lecker (Lit., ass-licker; taboo)

Person with a sweet tooth Nasher

Person with fine taste Feinshmeker

Pervert Faigeleh (taboo)

Pest Tsutsheppenish, nudnik

Pesty nagger Nudnik, onshikenish, tsutsheppenish

Petulant Baroyges, umgeduldik, kochedik

Philanthropist Baltsedokeh, filantrop; nadven (Hebrew)

Philanthropy (spirit of) Tsedokeh

Phylacteries Tefillen, tfillen (worn by observant Jews on head and left arm each weekday morning while praying)

Piece Shtik

Piece of luck Glick, mazel

(A) Piece of shit Shtik drek (taboo)

Pig Chazzer

135

Piggish person Chazzer (slang)

Pig's feed Chazzerei; also, slang for food unfit to eat or merchandise unworthy to buy or own

Pins and needles Shpilkes

Pious Frum (frimer)

Pious person Tsaddik, opgehitehner, shoimer mitzves

Piss (taboo) Pishechtz

(To) Piss (taboo) Pishen

(A) Pitiable person Nebach, nebechel, nebbish

Pity Rachmones

(A) Plague Makeh, finsternish, magaifeh

(To) Plague Tshepen, tshepen zich tsu

(A) Plague on you! A magaifeh zol dich trefen! A choleryeh ahf dir!

Play Shtik, drameh, pyesseh

Played-out person, even if young; a person unwilling to participate Alter kucker; oisgeputtert mentsh

Playgirl Tsatskeh, tsatskeleh

Plaything Tsatskeh, tsatskeleh (female)

Pleasantly plump and pretty (woman) Zaftik

Please Zeit zich matriach; zeit azoy gut; bitteh; zeit moichell

Please; I beg you. Ich bet eich.

Please forgive me. Zeit (mir) moychel.

Please keep quiet! Sha! (gently said)

(A) Pleasure! A fargenigen!

Pleasure (from children) Naches

Plump (woman) Zaftik

Policeman (slang) Shammes (actually a synagogue sexton)

Pompous woman Rebitsin (Lit., the Rabbi's wife)

Poor box Pushkeh (In every traditional Jewish home odd coins are put in this, particularly on Friday afternoon, before the Sabbath begins)

Poorhouse Hekdish

Poor man Orehman

Porridge Kasheh

Portable table Ruktish

(The) Posterior Toches! also tokus, tokis, tuckus, hinten (taboo)

136

Pot to defecate in Kuckteppel (taboo)

Pouting Ongeblozzen

Poverty Oremkeit

Powerhouse! A yung mit bainer!

(To) Pray Davenen

Prayer book daily in use Sidder

Prayer of mourner Kiddish

Prayer shawl Tallis

Pregnant Shvengert, trogedik

Pretend Kloymersht

Pretends to be ignorant of fact Macht zich nit visindik

Prettier ones they bury! (The girl is ugly!) Sheners laigt men in drerd arein.

Pretty girl Shaineh maidel; tshatshkeh (slang)

Pride (unreasonable and stubborn) Shtolt, Gav'aveh

Prima donna Prietskeh, pritseteh

Princess Bas-malkeh, printsesn

Privileged character Yachsen

Procrastinating! (Manana!) Kum ich nit heint, kuim ich morgen!

Profane Grob

Proper Kosher (slang)

Property Balebatishkeit

Proscription against wearing clothes that are mixed of wool and linen Shatnes

Prostitute Nafkeh, kurveh, nekaiveh, zoineh

Proverb Shprichvort (pl., sprichverter); gleichvort, gleichvertel

Puffed up (peeved) Ongeblozzen

Puffed up with haughty pride Geshvollen, ongeblozzen, blozen fun zich

(To) Pull Shlepen

Pun Vortshpiel

Punch Chmalyeh, klop, zetz, shmeiss, patsh, frask

(A) Punk Paskudnyak

Push Shtup (also used for sexual intercourse; taboo)

Put up or shut up! Toches ahfen tish!

Question   Frageh, sheileh
Quick, quickly   Shnell
Quiet, don't get excited!   Shat, shat! Hust!
Quiet! Stop talking!   Shveig! Shush!
Quiet! Shut up!   Sha! (shouted)
Quietly   Shtilinkerhait
Quite a job!   Folg mich a gahng!
Quite well   Gants gut, nishkosheh
Quorum of ten worshippers for praying   Minyan, minyo

R

Rabbi Rav, Rov, Rev

"Rabbi dear!" Rebiniu

Rabbi's wife Rebitsin

Rabid fan (also an ardent participant) Farbrenter; chosid

Racketeer Untervelt mentsh, gazlen (slang); ganef, goniff

Rag Shmatteh, tranteh

Raise cain Hulyen

To) Rape Trenen (taboo)

Rare thing Naidlecheh zach; zeltenkeit

Rarity An ain un aintsikeh

Rascally know-it-all Kolboynik

Ravioli Kreplech

Ready cash Mezuma

Real article; the real McCoy! Richtiker chaifetz

Real bargain! Billik vi borsht! (Lit., Cheap as beet soup)

Real buy! Billik vi borsht! (Cheap as beet soup)

Real fine, honorable man Mentsh

Really a bargain Tahkeh a metsieh, shoin ainmol a metsieh

Really crazy Meshugeh ahf toyt
Really! Is that so? Takeh? Azoy?
Rear Hinten
Rear parts Hinten
Recite prayers over lit candles Bentsh lecht; bentshe licht
Recite the afternoon prayers Davenen mincheh
Rectum Toches (taboo)
Relative through marriage (in laws) Mechuten (pl., mechutonim)
Relatives Mishpocheh, kroivim
Religious Frum (frimer)
Religious dietary law Kashress
Religious functionary who performs the circumcision Mohel
Remember? Gedainkst?
(To) Rent Dingen
Respect Koved, derech erets
Respectable Jews Balebatisheh yiden
Responsible Balebatish, achrahyes, farantvortlech
Reverence Koved, derech eretz
Rich Reich
Rich man G'vir
(To) ridicule Choyzik machen
Right Richtik; kosher (slang)
Righteous person Tsaddik
(To) Rip Trenen
Ritual bath (part of the orthodox bride's wedding preparation) Mikeveh
Ritual slaughterer of animals and fowl Shochet
Robber Gazlen, ganef
Robot Goilem
Rogue Yungatsh
Roisterer Tumler
Rotten (decayed) Farfoylt
Rotten person Paskudnik, paskudnyak
Rough Grob
Roughneck Shtarker, yungatsh; (sarcastically, voiler yung)

140

Round dumpling (usually made of matzoh meal, served with soup) K'naidel (pl., k'naidlech)

Row of pews at the eastern wall of the synagogue where the foremost members of the congregation sit Mizrach

Rude Grob

Rude, coarse person Bulvan, grober yung

Rude young man Grober yung

To) Ruin you Machen a tel fun dir

To be) Ruined Verren a tel

Rush! Elt zich!

Rustic Yishuvnik

Sabbath (twists of white) bread   Challeh
Sacrifice of atonement   Kaporeh
Sad sack!   Shmulky!
Salmon (smoked)   Lax, lox
(The) Same to you!   Gam atem! (Hebrew)
(A) Sap   Shnook
Satisfactory   Nishkosheh
Savory   Varnitshkes
Say a few words   Zog a por verter
(A) Saying   Gleichvertel
Scamp   Yungatsh
Scatterbrain   Draikop
Scholar   Lamden, ben toyreh
School   Shule
Scram!   Trog zich up! Avek!
Scrambled eggs   Feinkuchen
Scream   K'vitsh
Screech   K'vitsh
Screwy   Tsedrait
Scroll or the Book of Esther   Megillah
Second rater   Shlumpf

Self-made fool Shmok (taboo because it also means penis)

Senile Aiver butel, oiver botel

Sensuous looking (girl) Zaftik

Sentimental Shmaltzy, sentimentahl

Serpent Shlang (also big penis, taboo)

Serves him right! Gut oyf im! A shaineh, raineh, kaporeh!

Sexton of the synagogue Shamas, shammes

Sexual experience Zetz (taboo)

Sexual intercourse Shtup (taboo)

Sexually attractive girl Tzatzkeh, zaftik, zaftikeh moid

(To) Shake and dance with joy Hetskentzich, tzitern fun fraid

Shame and disgrace Mies un mos; a shandeh un a charpeh

Sharp (referring to clothes) Yontevdik

Sharp practices Genaivisheh shtiklech

She doesn't stop talking Zi farmacht nit dos moyl

She has all the virtues Aleh meiles hot zi

She should rest in peace. Oleho hasholom.

Shit Drek (taboo)

(To) Shit Kucken (taboo)

Shit-head Kucker, shitik drek (both taboo)

Shitty Farkacht, fefuckteh (taboo)

Shmohawk Anglicized variant for shmok (penis)

Shoddy Opgekrocken, shlak

Shoddy merchandise Opgekrocheneh schoireh, shlak vareh

(To) Shout for help Machen a g'vald

Shove Shtup, shtuppen

(You should) Shove it up your rectum Zolst es shtupin in toches arein! (taboo)

Shove (or stick) it up your rectum! Shtup es in toches! (taboo)

(A) Show-off K'nacker, grois-halter, barimer, shvitser

Shrew Shlecht veib; klipeh, mirshaas

Shriek Kvitsh

Shut up! Sha! Shveig! Farmach dos moyl!

Shy Shemevdik

143

Shy person Nebbish, nebechel, schemevdiker

Sick Krank

Sickness Krenk, krank-heit, cholaas

Sickness that hangs on Farshlepteh krenk

Silence! Zol zein shtil!

Simple-minded Tamavateh

Simple people Prosteh leit, prosteh mentshen

Simpleton Nebbish, shlemiel, shmendrik, tam

Sister-in-law Shvegerin

Sit in mourning Zitsen shiveh (Shiveh means seven—
the number of days in the mourning period)

Sit on pins and needles Zitsen ahf shpilkes.

Skilled worker Balmelocheh

Skin someone alive Reisen di hoit, shinden di hoit

Skinny Oysgedarcht

Skol Le'cha-yim, lechei-im, l'chei-im

*Skull cap usually worn during prayers and worn at all
times by extreme Orthodox Jews—also worn by
Catholic prelates* Yarmelkeh

Slam Chmalyeh

Slap (open hand Patsh; (back of the hand) Frassk

(To) Slap Geben a patsh

Slattern Yachneh

Sleeveless shirt (religious undershirt) Leibtzudekel,
tallis koton, arbeh kanfess

Slightly drunk Farshnoshket

Slime Shmuts

Slipshod worker or player (sports) Patsher

Slob Zhlob

Sloppy Ongepatshket

Slow Pamelech, pavolveh, gemitlech

Slowly Pamelech, pavolyeh, gemitlech

Slowpoke Kam vos er kricht

Slow-wittedness Goyisher kop; kunyehlemel

Slumhouse Churveh

Small pieces Shtiklech

Small pieces of baked dough Taiglech

*Small pockets of dough filled with chopped meat (like ra-
violi) or cheese* Kreplech

Smell Shmek; also plural for shmok, penis (taboo)

144

Smelled bad (used only in reference to food) Shtark gehert; ge'avert

(To) Smell bad Farshtunken, shtinken

Smoked salmon Lox (pronounced "lahks")

Snack (between meals) Nash

Snake Shlang, (also, big penis; taboo)

(The) Sneeze confirmed the truth. G'nossen tsum emess; Genossen oifn emmes!

Snored Gechropet

So? Well? Nu?

So, so! (evasive reply to So?) Nu, nu!

So I guessed wrong. Nisht getrofen!

So I made a mistake, so what? Host du bei mir an avleh!

So it goes. Azoy gait es.

So now? Ober yetzt? Ober itzt?

So soon? Azoy gich?

So you say! Vais ich vos!

So what! Host du bei mir an avleh!

Social background Yichus

Social climber Er kricht in di hoyecheh fenster.

Society Chevreh; farein

Soiled Shmutsik

(To) Soldier on the job Patshkeh

Someone else's Yenems

Something decorative (like a woman) Putskeh

Something delicious Mecheiehdik

Something unattainable Telerel fun himmel

Son Ben (Hebrew); Zun (Yiddish)

Son-in-law Aidim

Sorrel grass soup Shtshav, tshav

Sorrow Fardross

Soul Neshomeh

Soul condemned to wander for a time in this world because of its sins Dybbuk

Sour cream Smetteneh

Sour leaves soup Shtshav, tshav

(To be) Sparing Zhaleven

(To) Speak through your nose (unclear) Fonfen

(A) Speaker's fluff, an error Ponf

Social bit of acting Shpilen shtik, rolleh

Spinach soup   Shtshav, botshvineh

Spinster   Alteh moid

Spirit   Neshomeh

Spirit of philanthropy   Tsedokeh

Spitefully   Ahf tsi lehaches; tsuloches

Split your guts!   Plats!

Spoiled   Kalyeh

Sponger (beggar)   Shnorrer; (a hanger-on) Shlepper, onshikenish, tsutshepenish

(A) Squealer   Mosser

Squirt   Pisher (taboo)

Stacked (referring to a girl)   Zaftik

Stammerer   Ikevater, hikevater

Star of David   Mogen David

Start!   Fang shoyn on!

Starved   Toit hungerik

Steam bath   Shvitz bod

(A) Stink   Ipish, geshtank

(To) Stink   Shtinken

(It) Stinks!   Se shtinkt!

Stinky   Farshtunken (adj.), farshtunkener (noun)

Stockbroker   Mekler

Stomach ache   Boych vaitik

Stop annoying me.   Drai mir nit kain kop! Kush mich in toches (taboo, Lit., Kiss my behind)

Stop bending my ear!   Hak mir nit in kop!

Stop talking!   Shveig!

Stop talking yourself into illness!   A lung un leber ahf der noz!

Store that sells cheap, inferior merchandise, second-hand or cut-rate goods where bargaining over prices is important   Shlak joint (Americanism)

(A) Strange death!   A meisseh meshuneh! (Fig., It shouldn't happen to a dog!)

Stranger   Fremder

Street urchin (street Arab)   Yungatsh; arumloifer

Strong   Kreftik, shtark

Strong as a horse   Shtark vi a ferd

Strong-arm character   Shtarker

Strong character   Shtarker charakter

Strongly built person   A yung mit bainer!

Stubborn   Eingeshpart; akshen

Student of rabbinical academy   Yeshivah bocher

Stuff and nonsense!   Vais ich vos!

Stuffed cabbage   Holishkes, holubtshes, holebshess

Stuffed chicken-neck skin   Gefilteh helsel

Stuffed derma   Kishkeh (looks like sausage)

Stuffed fish   Gefilteh fish (usually made of chopped fish, onions and seasoning, and cooked in salt water)

Stuffed potato cakes   Varnishkes, varnitshkes

Stuffed shirt   Ongeblozzener

Stuffed up   Farshtopt, ongeshtopt

Substance   Balebatishkeit, iker, mamoshes

Sucker   Shlumpf, shnook, yold

Suckered!   Opgeflickt!

Suddenly   In miten drinen; miten derinnen

(To) Suffer   Plagen zich, leiden

Suffix to denote diminutive or affection   El, eleh

Summer boarding house with cooking privileges   Kochalain

Super-sensitive   Aidel gepatshkit

Superb (in taste)   Mecheiehdik

(To) Sweat out a job   Plagen zich, mutshen zich

Sweaty   Shlumpy (Americanism), farshvitst

Sweet cake   Shtrudel

Sweet carrot compote   Tsimmes

Sweet soul   Ziseh neshomeh

Sweet talk   Shmaltz, ziseh raidelech

Sweet thing   Ziskeit

Sweetheart   Neshomeleh! Tei-yerinkeh! Hartseniu!

Sweetness   Ziskeit

Swill   Chazzerei

(To) Swindle   Shmeikel

Swindler   Ganef, shvindler

Swollen up; puffed up (applied to person with haughty pride)   Geshvollen

Synagogue   Shul, bes medresh

T.O.T. See Toches ahfen tish

Tact Saichel, takt, manyeren

Tail Shvontz (also refers to a man who behaves ungallantly or idiotically)

Tailor Shneider

Take it! Na!

Take it easy! Chap nit! also, Me ken nit tantzen ahf tsvai chassenes mit ain mol!

(To) Take pains Zich matriach zein

(To) Take trouble Zich matriach zein

Tale bearer Shalatten-shammes

(To) Talk (idly) Shmoozen, shmuessen

Talk oneself into sickness Zich einreden a krenk

Talk to the wall (to talk in vain or to talk and receive no answer) Red tsu der vant

Talk your heart out Me redt zich oys dos hartz

Talkative woman Yenteh, klaperkeh

Talking for the sake of talking Haken a tseinik

Talking through the nose Reden fonfevateh; fonfen

Talking yourself into illness! Zich einreden a krenk; zich einreden a lung un lebber ahf der noz!

Tall story Bobbeh meisseh; nit geshtoigen

Talmudic academy Yeshiva

Taste   Ta'am

Tasty   Geshmak

Tea   Tai; glezel tai; glezeleh varems

Teacher   Melamed, lehrer

Teamaster   Balagoleh

(To) Tear   Trenen, reisen

Teats   Tsitskes (taboo); bristen

Teen-ager   (female) Maidel, maideleh; (male) Yingel;
   boytshik; boytshikel (Americanism)

(To) Tell a lie   Zogen a ligen

(A) Terrible thing   Gevaldikeh zach, shreklecheh zach

Testicles   Baitsim (taboo)

Thank God!   Danken Got! Got tsu danken!

Thank you!   A dank! A shainen dank!

Thanks for a small favor.   A gezunt in dein pupik.

Thanks for nothing.   A shainem dank in pupik.

That's all   Dos iz alts

That's enough!   Shoyn genug!

That's how it goes.   Azoy gait es.

That's how it is.   Azoy iz es.

That's how the cookie crumbles!   Azoy vert dos kichel
   tzekrochen!

That's it!   Dos iz es!

That's nothing.   Ez iz bloteh.

That's what you say!   Azoy zugstu! (sing.) Azoy zugt ir!
   (pl.)

That's worthless   Es iz bloteh. Es iz drek. (taboo)

The business (slang)   Shmeer

The devil with him!   Zol er gaien tsu alleh ruaches!

The faster the better   Vos gicher, alts besser

The good old days   Mehlech sobieskis yoren (Lit., the
   years of King Sobieski); In di alteh guteh tseiten

The hell with him!   A brand oif im! Kuck im on! (taboo)

The hell with it!   Ich hob es in drerd! Zol es brennen!

The marriage is off!   Oys shiddech!

The majority rules!   Az drei zogen meshugeh, darf der
   ferter zogen "Bim bom." Az dos velt zogt shikker, laigt
   men zich shlofen.

The nuisance is here already!   Er iz shoyn du, der nudnik!

The real McCoy! Richtiker chaifetz! Di emmeseh schoireh!

The sneeze confirmed the truth. G'nossen oyfen emess.

The whole works (slang) Shmeer, megillah

Then Den

There's a buzzing in my head! Es zhumit mir in kop!

There is not Nito

There still is Es iz noch do

They don't let you live. Me lost nit leben.

They say Me zogt

They talk and talk and say nothing. Me redt, me redt un me shushkit zich.

Thief Goniff, ganef

This pleases me. Dos gefelt mir.

This too is a living! (This you call a living?) Oych mir a leben!

This was a pleasure! Dos is geven a mecheieh!

This will do. Es vet kleken.

Thrown-out money Aroysgevorfen gelt

Thumb Grober finger

Tickle Kitsel

Tightwad Karger

Tiny Pitsel, pitseleh

Tired Farmatert

Tired out Oysgematert, ongematert, farmatert

(To do all the) Talking A braiteh daieh hoben

(To have no end of) Trouble Hoben tsu zingen un tsu zogen (Lit., To have to sing and to talk)

To life! Le'chayim! Lechi-yim!

To your health! Le'chayim! Lechei-yim!

Toes Fisfinger, shpitsfinger

Too bad! Az och un vai!

Too bad (novel complaint) that the bride is too pretty A chissoren di kaleh iz tsu shain

Too costly Tsufil, tsi tei'er

Too dear Tsufil, tsu tei'er

Too late Noch ne-ileh! Tsu shpait!

Too much Tsufil

Tough guy Shtarker; k'nacker

Tough luck! Az och un vai!

Toy (doo-dad) Tshatshki, tsatskeh

Traditional higher school Yeshiva

Tragedy Umglick, tragedyeh

Travel in good health! For gezunterhait!

Treasury of Jewish law, interpreting the Torah (five books of Moses) into livable law Talmud

(A) Treat (food) Meichel, nash

Tremendous purchase (bargain) Metsieh

Tricks Shtiklech, kuntzen

Trickster Mamzec, draikop, opnarer

Tricky doings Gehnaivisheh shtiklech

Trifles Shmontses, bobkes, bubkes

Triflings Shmontses, bobkes, bubkes

Trouble-maker Er kricht oyf di gleicheh vent

Troubles Tsores (sing., tsoreh)

Troublesome wife Shlang (slang, also means penis—taboo); shlecht veib; shlok

Truth Emmis, emmes

Tub Vaneh

Ugly   Mies
Ugly thing or person   Mieskeit
Unattainable   Telerel fun himmel
Unconscious   Chaloshes
Uncouth person   Grober, grober mentsh, grobyan, gru-
   byan
Uncouth young man   Grober yung
Underwear (long, winter)   Gatkes
(An) Unfortunate   Kalyekeh
Ungraceful person   Klotz
Unhurried   Gemitlich
Unkempt   Shlumpy, shlumperdik
Unlucky one   Shlimazel
(An) Unlucky person is a dead person   A mentsh on glik
   iz a toyter mentsh
Unlucky, pitiable person   Nebach, shlimazel, nebbishel,
   nebachel
Unmarried girl   Maidel (young one); moid (older one);
   b'suleh (virgin)
Unmarried man   Bocher
Unnecessary   Nisht, naitek

152

Unpalatable food Chazzerei, men ken es in moil nit nemen

Unsteady Shvindeldik, shokeldik

Untidy person Shlump, shlumper

Untrustworthy person Mamzer, draikop

Unwanted (companion or) follower Noch-shlepper; tsutsheppenish; onshikenish

Uproar Tumel

Upstart Oyfgekumener

(To) Urinate Pishen

Urinator Pisher (taboo, derogatory term applied to adult; affectionately applied to infant)

Urine Pishechtz (taboo)

Utter misery Gehakteh tsores; gebrenteh tsores

Vagina Loch, peeric, pirgeh, k'nish (all taboo)
Very little A biseleh
(A) Very poor man Kabtzen in ziben poless
Very wealthy (slang) Ongeshtopt; ongeshtopt mit gelt
Vicious animal (usually refers to an inhuman person)
    Baizeh chei-eh
Virgin B'suleh
Virginity K'nippel, b'sulehshaft
Virtue Meileh
(To) Visit Kumen tsu gast; gaien tsu gast
Vulgar Prost; grobyungish
Vulgar man (one without manners) Balagoleh, prostak,
    proster mentsh
Vulgar people Prosteh leit, prosteh mentshen, pros-
    taches

Wail of sorrow   G'vald!

Wait   Vart

Walk on toes   Gain oif di shpitsfinger

Wallop   Klop, shmeis, zetz, chmalyeh

(To) Wander (to be lost)   Blonjen

(To) Wander around aimlessly   Valgeren zich, voglen

Wandered around   Arumgevolgert; arumgevalgert

Washroom   Vashtsimmer

Watch out (to mind)   Varfen an oyg

Watch yourself as if a fire threatened!   Hit zich vi fun a feier!

Watchman   Shoymer, vechter

We shall say grace.   Mir vellen bentshen.

We try harder!   Mir bamien zich shtarker!

We'll bury him!   Mir velen im bagroben!

Weakling   Nebbish, nebachel, k'vatsh

Weakness   Chaloshes (faintness); shvachkeit

Wealth   Reich

(Very) Wealthy (slang)   Ongeshtopt (overly stuffed)

Wear it in good health!   Trog es gezunterhait!

Wee (very small)   Pitsel, pitseleh

Well?   Nu?

155

Well done! Well said! A leban ahf dein kop! (complimentary)

Well said! Zaier shain gezogt! Gut gezogt!

What a . . . ! Sara . . . !

What a sober man has on his mind (lung), a drunkard has on his tongue. Vos bei a nichteren oyfen lung, iz bei a shikkeren oyfen tsung.

What are they lacking? Vos felt zai?

What are you bothering me for? Vos draist mir dem kop?

What are you saying? Vos zogt ir?

What are you fooling around for? Vos barist du?

What are you screwing around for? Vos barist du? (taboo)

What are you talking about? Vos ret ir epes?

What are you talking my head off for? Vos hakst du mir in kop?

What did I need it for? Tsu vos hob ich dos gedarft?

What difference does it make? Vos macht dos oys? Vos iz der chil'lek?

What difference does it make as long as he makes a living? Nifter-shmifter, a leben macht er? (Lit., "nifter" means dead)

What difference does it make to me? Vos macht es mir oys?

What do I care? Vos art es mich?

What do you hear around? Vos hert zich?

What does it lead to? Vos iz der tachlis?

What does it matter (to me)? Vos art es (mich)? *(to you)?* Vos art eich? S'art eich?

What does it mean? Vos maint es?

What else? Vo den? Vos noch?

What is the name of . . . ? Vi ruft men . . . ? Vi hais es . . . ?

What is the trick? Vos iz di chochmeh?

What kind of a . . . ? Sara . . . ?

What matters it to you? S'art eich? Vos art es eich?

What then? Vo den? Vos noch?

What will be? (Que sera?) Vos vet zein

What's cooking? Vos tut zich? Vos kocht zich in teppel?

156

What's going on? Vos tut zich?

What's new? Vos hert zich epes neies?

What's on his mind is on his tongue Vos ahfen lung iz ahfen tsung

What's the matter? Vos iz?

What's the outcome? Vos iz di untershteh shureh?

What's the point? Vos iz di untershteh shureh?

What's the purpose? Vos iz der tachlis?

What's the trick? Vos iz di chochmeh?

What's wrong with you? Vos iz mit dir? Vos felt dir?

What's your name? Vi haistu? Vi ruft men eich?

When I eat, they can all go to hell! Ven ich ess, hob ich zai alleh in drerd.

When people talk about something, it is probably true. Az es klingt, iz misstomeh chogeh.

Where are you going? Vuhin gaistu? Vu gaistu?

Where does it hurt you? Vu ut dir vai?

Where the devil says "good morning" Vu der ruach zogt "gut morgen"

Whine K'vetsh, klogen

(A) Whiner A k'vetsher, a k'vatsh, a k'vetsh

Whirring noise Zhumet, zhumerei

Whiskey Bronfen, shnapps, mashkeh

(A) Whisper Shushkeh

(To) Whisper Shushken zich

Who knows! Freg mir becherim! (slang); Ver vaist? (Lit.)

Who would have believed it? Ver volt dos geglaibt?

Whom are you fooling? Vemen baristu? Vemen narstu?

Whom are you kidding? Vemen baristu?

Whore Kurveh, nafkeh, nekaiveh

Whorehouse Bordel, shandhoiz, nafkeh bayis

Whoremaster Yentzer

Why should I do it? Folg mich a gang! (sarcastically)! Farvos zol ich es tun? (Lit.)

Wider than longer Braiter vi lainger

Wife of a chazen Chazenteh

Wife of a melamed Melamedkeh

Wife of a rabbi Rebitsin

Wig Shaitel, (sheitel)

Wild Jewish boy Shaigetz, tsevildeveter
Wild Jewish girl Shikseh, vildeh moid
(A) Wild man! A vilder mentsh!
(A) Wild one! A vilder mentsh!
(To) Win gin rummy game without opponent scoring Shneider (Colloquial)
Wisdom Chochmeh
Wisecrack Gleichvertel
(A) Wise guy K'nacker, chochem, chochem attick
Wise man Chochem
(To) Wish lots of trouble on someone A miesseh meshuneh!
Witch Machashaifeh
Without means (poor) Orehman
Witticism Gleichvertel (also used sarcastically), chochmeh
Woe! Vai!
Woe be to it! Och un vai!
Woe is me! Oi! Vai is mir! A klug iz mir! A broch tsu mir!
Woman in labor Kimpetoren
Woman of great beauty Yefayfiyeh; shainkeit
Woman prayer leader Zogerkeh
(To) Work or play half-heartedly Patshkeh, patshken
(To) Work hard Plagen zich; mutshen zich; mordeven zich
Worked to death Oysgemutshet
(A) Worker who does a job insufficiently gives you A lek un a shmek
Working on Sabbath Mechalel Shabbes; shabbes goy.
World to come Yeneh velt; oilem habbo (Hebrew)
Worn out Oysgemahtert, farmutshet
Worried Fardeiget
Worthless Gornit vert; shkapeh, bobkes, tinif (all slang); chei kuck! (taboo)
Worthless clothing Shmatteh; tranteh
Would that it come true! Alevai! Halevai!
Wound Makeh, vund
Wretch Shlak, shlok
Wrong Kalyeh, shlecht

Yearly remembrance of the dead   Yorzeit
You already forgot?   Host shoyn fargessen?
You can burst?   Me ken tsezetzt veren!
You can go crazy!   Me ken meshugeh veren!
You can vomit from this!   Me ken brechen fun dem!
You can't dance at two weddings simultaneously.   Me ken nit tantzen ahf tsvai chassenes inainem.
You can't get rid of it.   Me ken nit poter veren!
You don't frighten me!   Gai shtrasheh di gens! Mich shrekt men nit!
You don't have to be pretty if you have charm.   Me darf nit zein shain; me darf hoben chain.
You don't show a fool something half-finished.   A nar veist men nit kain halbeh arbet.
You fool, you!   Nar ainer!
You ought to be ashamed of yourself!   Shemen zolstu zich in dein veiten haldz!
You please me a great deal.   Ir gefelt mir zaier.
You should choke on it!   Dershtikt zolstu veren!
You should get a stomach cramp!   Se zol dich chapen beim boych! Se zol dir grihmen in boych!

159

You should live (and be well)!   A leben ahf dir Zolst
   leben un zein gezunt!

You should live so!   Zolstu azoy laiben!

You should swell up like a mountain!   Zolst geshvollen
   veren vi a barg!

You shouldn't know from bad!   Zolst nit vissen fun kain
   shlechts.

You understand?   Farshtaist?

Young and old   Kind un kait; yung un alt

Young doll   Yingeh tsahtskeh; yefaiyfiyeh

(A) Young, vigorous lad   Yungermantshik, chevrehman

Youngest child in family   Mizinikil

You're all set!   Zeit ir doch ahfen ferd!

You're not making sense.   Nisht geshtoigen, nisht
   gefloigen.

You're welcome!   Nito farvos!

You're welcome (in my home).   Shmirt zich oys di
   shich.

Yummy-yummy;   Se tsegait zich in moyl!